RECLAIMING MY EDGE AFTER CANCER

RACHEL DESPAIN

Acknowledgments

I wrote this memoir for my precious daughter, Zoelle, who has filled my life with immense joy and color. Your compassion is unparalleled, and you are the fiercest protector of your loved ones. My hope is that you will pursue your passions, and love and protect yourself with the same vigor. You are enough and you are so loved, just the way you are. Being your mom is the greatest joy of my life.

I want to acknowledge three people without whom I simply wouldn't be here today:

First, I would like to thank my mom for instilling grit and fierce determination in me that fueled my perseverance through so many challenges in life. Your unconditional love kept the fire burning in me when I felt like giving up.

Next, I would like to thank my dad for providing an invaluable sounding board and inspiring me to see my full potential. Without you, I'm not sure if I would have been able to find my authentic voice or believe in myself.

And, finally, I would like to thank my husband Matt, the love of my life. Your endless love, humor, and companionship has buoyed me through some of life's greatest challenges. There is absolutely nobody else on the planet who could fill your gigantic shoes. I will be eternally grateful that you strapped yourself into this wild ride with me. You've made each day infinitely brighter.

There are so many people who've helped me throughout my tumultuous journey, especially my amazing cadre of girlfriends (and my Aunt Pam) who've weathered various parts of this voyage with me. You've been my lifeboat and kept me afloat through it all.

CONTENTS

For there is always light, if only we're brave enough to see it. If only we're brave enough to be it. ~Amanda Gorman

Riptide

With each step, I felt the grains of sand below my feet. The crashing of the waves softened as the tide went out, and I listened to the birds chirping while the sunrise deepened into a billowy fuchsia that enveloped the sky above me. In the two years since Mom passed away, my senses had dulled, and the sounds and colors of the world drained into a vacuous cloud surrounding me. Now it was as if my body was waking after a long, dreamless hibernation.

Zoe loved the ocean, so we were at the beach for spring break. I was inspired to be able to tap into feelings of joy and adventure that felt distantly familiar to me. I didn't want our daughter to remember me as sad and boring during those formative years.

That afternoon, I'd researched a long hike to a remote beach and gathered some gear for the family.

"Does anyone want to hike to a beautiful spot for a sunset swim?" I asked cheerily.

"Oh, you know it!" Zoe said, returning from a lizard hunt.

Matt looked down at me with a familiar smile. He loved these kinds of adventures: the ones that built the framework of a deep, unspoken connection between us, and he had been patiently waiting for that version of myself – the one he'd known before Mom died – to resurface.

The room filled with the hum of excitement for the possibilities ahead. I had longed for the feeling of spontaneity to return, and I couldn't wait to go exploring with my favorite people. As we locked the front door to our worn-out cabin, I noticed Zoe wasn't wearing shoes. I secretly loved this barefoot, up-for-anything spirit of hers, but we were heading out for an unfamiliar hike.

"Zoe Bear, shoes!" I yelled out, and finally we were on our way. Without any concept of time or any obligations to weigh us down, we sang and laughed through the first part of our walk, which was steep and heavily forested.

Midway through the hike, I felt a sharp, stabbing pain over my left breast. "Ow!" I yelled, a little too loudly, as I stopped and put my hand over my chest.

"What happened?" Matt asked, looking confused.

"I don't know." I chose my words carefully because our eight-year-old daughter was looking at me with deep concern. She was the worrier and protector in our little family unit, and I didn't want to concern her.

We continued walking for another five minutes, then I had to stop and sit down. The pain came back again. It was clearly sending me a message. I silently promised myself to get it checked out as soon as we got back home, and we went on to the beach, enjoying the rest of our trip as if nothing had happened.

When we got back to Austin, I called to schedule my routine mammogram. I recently had my annual exam with my OB/GYN, Dr.S. She performed a routine breast exam. Everything looked and felt normal, but I wanted to get the mammogram done right away for peace of mind. When I called, the receptionist asked if I had had any pain or concerns, or if this was this just a routine exam.

I paused and said, "Actually, yes. I have had some pain in my left breast recently, and for the past few weeks, I've felt like there's a rock in my left armpit."

"I would suggest that you hang up and call Dr. S," she replied. "Ask her to request a diagnostic mammogram instead of an ordinary one."

I did as she suggested and called my doctor, who immediately agreed and put in the request for the diagnostic mammogram that would also include an ultrasound.

I went in for my appointment, and first they completed the mammogram. Then I went into another room where an ultrasound tech named Bonnie sat down next to me to do my ultrasound.

"Everything looked clear and normal in your mammogram," she told me, "but we're doing the ultrasound as an extra step today since you were experiencing some symptoms." Her kindness and reassurance instantly put me at ease.

She spent about forty-five minutes with my ultrasound that day. Upon first glance, things looked pretty good, but she was thorough and kept going back and checking and re-checking each area. Finally, she took some photos and showed me that she found a suspicious spot on the ultrasound. She proceeded to check the lymph node area in my left armpit. Thankfully, that area appeared to be clear of any problems.

Bonnie instructed me to wait in another room where I would speak with the radiologist who would discuss the mass they had found on the ultrasound. When they called me back into the office, the doctor was very matter-of-fact. "As you know, we found a suspicious mass in your left breast. I would say it is moderately suspicious. We would like to get you scheduled for a biopsy right away so we can find out more."

"Okay. I'll be sure to do that," was all I was able to say before walking to the checkout area where I scheduled my biopsy for three days later.

When I was home with Matt, I told him we needed to talk. With its open floor plan, our house made it difficult to keep our private conversations from our daughter's curious ears, so we walked out onto the back patio. I explained to him that they had found a suspicious mass and recommended a biopsy.

"Okay, but that's pretty common, right?" he asked. I'd had one other suspicious mass that needed an ultrasound just after Zoe was born, and that had turned out to be nothing serious. "Right ..." I said hesitantly.

The morning of my biopsy, I left a little early to allow plenty of time to get to the office. Because it was a minor procedure and we wouldn't get the results that day, I decided to go alone. After parking at the office, I sat in the car for a few minutes to check my messages on my phone. While I was sitting there, someone driving a new Mercedes hit the back of my car. A doctor driving his wife's car, that he wasn't used to, misjudged the parking area and hit my car when he was trying to pull in. I barely noticed, and I didn't get out of my car until he walked up to my car to explain what happened. He was very kind and apologetic. My only question was whether he was going to be the one performing my biopsy that day. Clearly, my mind was so focused on the procedure that I didn't even care that someone hit my car. I was glad to find out that he wasn't doing my procedure because I didn't want anything to rattle the nerves of the doctor doing the biopsy that day.

I nervously went inside, and the doctor performed the biopsy. The doctor inserted a needle inside my breast where the ultrasound technician showed him the lump was located. He took a couple samples of my tissue, then he inserted a titanium clip that marked the area for future tracking. I was still anxious and eager to get the results back from my biopsy, but I felt a huge weight of relief lift from my shoulders when the procedure was done. They told me I would receive the results within three days, and Dr. S had already explained to me that if everything was fine, she would call me. If there was a problem, she would schedule an appointment for me to come in to discuss it.

Three days later, I received a call from the office asking if I could come in the following morning to go over the results. I said yes, and this time Matt insisted on coming with me. Dr. S – a lovely doctor who I knew and trusted – walked in quietly without the warm smile that normally greeted me. She sat down and said, "Rachel, unfortunately, you have breast cancer."

I felt her eyes on me as she waited for my response. "I knew it," I finally said.

For some reason, it's uncommon to feel pain from a lump in your breasts or lymph nodes that have been affected by breast cancer, but I had definitely been feeling pain in mine. Deep down, I had known something was wrong, and my initial feeling after receiving the diagnosis was relief. I felt so grateful for each step that had been properly executed to bring me to that moment because there were so many opportunities for errors. What if I had put off the appointment for another year? What if I hadn't received the additional ultrasound or someone less thorough had performed it? What if the doctor who performed my biopsy made an error? What if the doctors who evaluated my biopsy hadn't found my cancer? There were so many what ifs, and I was grateful to have the information I needed to take this on.

Dr. S went on to explain that this appeared to be a stage 1 estrogen positive (ER+) progesterone positive (PR+) invasive ductal carcinoma (IDC). Basically, this is the most common form of breast cancer, and it's fed by estrogen. It appeared to be slow growing, and Dr. S comforted me by saying if there is a type of breast cancer to get, it would be the one I had. She said I would need an oncologist, and I would most likely need surgery and chemotherapy.

My only question for her was "Is it normal to have a clear mammogram and find the cancer through an ultrasound?" She paused before replying

"Not really. That's not very common."

We walked out, and I noticed the color had drained from Matt's face. He gave me a big hug, though, and we stood there quietly for a couple minutes.

Looking down at me, he said, "I feel like I'm more upset about this than you are."

I was in a state of shock, unable to process my own emotions. After a lifetime of suppressing my feelings, I realized how strange it was that my own fear and anxiety were so deeply buried beneath the surface that I couldn't even tell they were lurking below. My mind was fully focused on getting better and making sure that my family was going to be okay. I didn't leave any space for myself to grieve this awful diagnosis. I realized in that moment that I had more to worry about than just cancer. I needed to learn how to prioritize myself and allow my feelings to surface so I could work through them.

Damn, there's a longer road ahead of me than I want to believe.

When I got home, I called my family and friends to share the news with them. Magically, I'd somehow morphed into a superhero overnight. Everyone was calling me a "Warrior" and saying, "You've got this!"

After I got off the phone and sat alone for a while, what I felt like, deep down, was exactly the opposite of a Warrior. I may have looked and sounded strong to everyone, but deep inside I felt sad, scared, and weak. I just wanted to curl up on the couch and cry, but I wasn't even tuned into my feelings enough to allow that to happen. I could sense those feelings stirring deep below the surface. Not only did I have cancer, but now I began to feel the burden of pressure from all of my loved ones to be strong and beat cancer. First, I knew I had to give myself the space I needed to process my own emotions over this life changing diagnosis. I quickly realized there was no time for carrying the weight of others' expectations of me.

Crisis has a way of inherently sifting out things that don't matter and illuminating the best path forward. When I woke up the next morning, I had some newfound clarity. I was in a riptide, and I fully respected the danger of the situation I was facing. I could futilely try to fight and control the strong current swiftly taking me out to sea, or I could stay calm and realize that cancer wasn't going to take me under. It was pulling me away from my shore, but I wasn't going to drown.

Owning our story can be hard but not nearly as difficult as spending our lives running from it. ~Brene' Brown

A Wild Ride

As I peered down the hood of our silver Thunderbird, I could tell we were swerving more dramatically. My heart pumped with fear as the radio blared Mom's favorite Abba song, but the lyrics were providing me with imaginary strength.

"Do we have any plans for tomorrow?" I asked, tapping Mom's leg, trying to make small talk with her to keep her awake.

"Hmm," was all she could muster.

Then I saw an exit from the highway approaching, so I slid over next to her, putting my arms in front of her. "Mom, pull over! Take this exit now!"

She was leaning back in her seat, and I realized that I needed to take over. I put my hand on the steering wheel and turned it to the right – a little too hard. The car went onto the shoulder of the road, and we almost hit the guardrail.

"Mom, slow down!" I may have been able to help steer, but I had no control over the speed of the car. I was trying to guide the wheel toward the exit to our right, but I pulled the wheel too hard. I heard a loud thud under the car as we drove into a ditch on the access road next to the highway, and I flew forward and hit the dashboard. The car came to a sudden stop.

My heart was beating so fast and hard I thought it was going to burst out of my chest. *We're not dead. I can't believe it,* were the first thoughts that came to mind when I opened my eyes again. Mom had fallen over sideways on the bench seat , so I shook her to see if she could wake up. I was terrified that a police officer was going to find us there. I was relieved that neither of us were hurt, but Mom needed to pull it together. I shook her wildly, and she turned her head to the side and vomited all over the seat and the floorboard. I couldn't get her to respond.

I sat there quietly in the car for another five or ten minutes, trying to figure out what to do next. I realized I had to get out of the car. I could see a gas station ahead, the bright lights were a welcome oasis from the quiet, dark stretch of road in Austin that night. Finally, I summoned the courage to go there to get help. If I stayed in the car with Mom, she could get arrested, and who knew what would happen to me. Those thoughts inspired me to make a move.

Resigned to my plan, I was shocked to discover my legs felt numb and shaky. I had to use my hands to move my legs into the right position to get out. Once I was out of the car, and had gathered my strength, a resolve came over me. It was my job – mine alone – to get us out of this situation.

I ran to the gas station and swung the door open, determination flooding through me. I was not afraid. The attendant looked up at me and didn't say anything at first.

I walked up to the counter. "Can I please get a cup of water?"

She looked at me carefully, then she looked back at the door as if waiting to see whether someone else was with me. I guess it wasn't normal for a ten-year old kid to come into a gas station alone at that time of night.

"My mom is just down the street, and she's really sick. I need to get some water for her." I said, with increasing urgency.

"Oh, honey, let me help you," she said as she walked over to the beverage station and grabbed the largest Styrofoam cup available.

She filled it with ice water and said, "You go on, but I'm here if you need anything."

I made my way back to the car, and when I opened the door, the reek of vomit stopped me in my tracks. Mom was still lying on her side, and a tug of panic took over.

"Mom, get up now! Mom! We have to go now. I need you to get up!"

Still nothing.

I ripped the lid off the cup and poured half the cup of ice-cold water over Mom's head. She grunted and opened her eyes. "Stop," she muttered.

I handed her the cup. "I need you to drink this," I said, pleading with her.

At first, she just leaned back on the seat, but after a few minutes she sat upright to take a sip. We sat there for what felt like an eternity until she drank some more. Finally, she started the car, and we slowly made our way back home.

The drive home that night felt like it would never end. Below the hard surface of my persistent fear, bubbles of resentment began floating up like the fizz in a bottle of Big Red. I began to realize that Mom chose to bring me along for the ride. I couldn't make peace with why she brought me with her on a night like that. *Is this what always happens when she is out with her friends,* I wondered? My fears deepened as the prickly, unwelcome feelings of resentment and doubt worked their way to the surface.

Mom got pregnant with me when she was sixteen and gave birth to me in San Antonio at the tender age of seventeen. My parents weren't exactly in love at the time and they definitely weren't planning to have a baby together. When I came along, they did what honorable southern kids did at the time; they got married. It was a struggle for them. I think Dad had bigger plans for himself than the reality of what our simple life offered, and Mom wasn't exactly ready to give up her social life and settle down either. Neither of them were ready for the curveball that my appearance threw their way.

Mom and Dad fought a lot, and they didn't really share the same values and interests. Considering how vastly different they were, they made it an impressive four years before they divorced. Regardless of the difficulties we experienced during that time, there were fleeting moments of joy. Mom's family loved kids and since I was the first grandchild on her side of the family, I was surrounded by love and attention in ways I had never known.

Mom and I moved into an apartment with her friend Kenyon and her son, Brad. Brad and I were about the same age, and we shared a room with two beds. Our parents had both recently divorced, so our moms made the most of the situation by sharing living expenses. Brad and I often played in nearby creeks, catching craw-dads. Having a friend and companion during those unstable times provided me with the comfort I needed to endure it and not feel so different from everyone else. We got by with a lot of help from Mom's parents and siblings, but money was definitely tight. Eventually, we moved to Austin where Mom worked long hours for a garbage company to make ends meet, and sometimes I slept on the floor of her office in my sleeping bag. We didn't have much, and sometimes I felt sorry for myself about that. Over time I realized how hard she had to work and how much she had to sacrifice to put a roof over our heads and healthy food on the table.

I looked forward to the occasional visits I had with my dad, but most of the time our weekends consisted of doing chores and following his normal routines. We would wash his 280Z, and I would sit on top of the amp while he and his band practiced their music. One time when I was in second or third grade, I got excited because he told me we were going to a movie and I thought maybe we could see something that I might have some interest in. He took me to see the Woody Allen movie *Annie Hall*. It felt as though he wanted me to be older and more mature than I was at the time and I felt like I was letting him down somehow by just being a normal kid and wanting to do normal-kid things.

Our visits just felt like he was continuing his normal routine as if I wasn't actually there and that was a tough pill to swallow. Sometimes in the evenings, he left me in his apartment while he went next door to play Monopoly with his friends. All I wanted at the time was his attention. I wanted him to take an interest in some things that I liked to do, like swimming and skating. My dad didn't seem to understand that, preferring to do his own thing and allow me to tag along as an afterthought. It was how differently we each wanted to spend our time together that left a scar on me.

I don't think Mom had the opportunity to enjoy being carefree for many years because she had to be the primary caretaker of a child when she was so young. After Dad left, Mom had to juggle working long hours while raising me on her own, and she also tried to squeeze in some fun when she could. She went out with her friends to the local icehouses, and sometimes she brought me out with her. I played video games while she and her friends sat around tables, drinking and listening to music. I enjoyed those days, growing up in the '70s in Austin. As an only child at the time, her friends gave me a lot of attention. They took turns giving me coins to buy Big Red or play pinball or Galaga. Sometimes I got lucky and another kid would show up and we ran around in the woods while the adults drank beer and two-stepped to the sounds of southern outlaw musicians like Willie Nelson and Waylon Jennings.

When I was in third grade, Mom had to fire a disgruntled employee. He broke into our duplex and left disturbing notes inside. He also left a dead snake on our lawn and other things meant to frighten us – at least Mom felt sure that he was the person behind these things – and his plan was working. We were scared so Mom finally called the police, who said that because nothing was stolen except for a picture of my mom, there wasn't much they could do. Mom decided to take matters into her own hands and asked a friend from work to sleep on the living room floor with a gun. I never slept very well during those times, and I often crawled into bed with Mom when I heard the slightest sound. I had a recurring nightmare for years afterwards that our house was being broken into, and it often woke me up in the middle of the night.

I loved my mom in a primal way that perhaps could only be understood by other kids in my position, except I didn't have any friends who were an "only child" of a single mom. We were so close, and I felt like it was my job to protect her from the world. I stayed up listening for sounds at night, and when Mom didn't come home when I expected her to, I sat for hours in the windowsill, waiting for her to return. I watched lightning bugs and other families playing together in their front yards as it grew dark.

I felt totally alone in those moments when Mom was not around. She said I wasn't allowed to tell anyone I was being left alone because she could get in trouble if they found out. There were no computers or cell phones back then to distract me, and late-night television often involved scary shows that made my anxiety deepen. So I did my best to bury my feelings of fear and anxiety and tell myself alternate truths like "maybe she got tired and decided to stay at her friend's house instead of risking the drive home" or "she just lost track of time". I would make any excuses for her that prevented me from dealing with the dark reality of the recurring situation I found myself in.

I treasured the times when Mom and I were together. We walked hand-in-hand to the grocery store or ice cream shop, singing our favorite songs together. No matter how broke we were, Mom went out of her way to make sure I had enough to make me feel special. She worked extra hours to make sure we had good food, normal clothes and occasional treats. Even though money was extremely tight and we lived in humble digs, she somehow managed to provide just enough to keep me from feeling like I was missing anything significant from a materialistic perspective.

In the summer after fourth grade, Mom decided to move back to San Antonio to live with my grandparents for a while so she could get her feet back on the ground financially. I think my nomadic seeds were planted at this early age as I came to realize if the circumstances around you are difficult, you can just change your environment instead of dealing with the circumstances directly. Mom's dad – I called him Paw-Paw – had been like a dad to me for most of my younger years. Paw-Paw was the one who drove to Austin to pick me up when it got late and Mom didn't come home. Paw-Paw took me fishing, camping, horseback riding and we often went on cross-country road trips together. He put in 8 track cassette tapes of Merle Haggard, and we sang in the front seat of his old turquoise Chevy pickup truck like nothing else mattered in the world.

(Left): Mom, Dad and I 1972. (Right): Me as a young child, 1975.

(Left): Me & Paw-Paw. (Right): Me & Paw-Paw's truck

How you love yourself is how you teach others to love you. ~Rupi Kaur

Bottle Rocket

Mom had a sister, Pam, and two brothers, Harold and Roy. My aunt and uncles often took turns watching me. Harold and Pam often took me to baseball and softball games. Paw-Paw coached softball and Pam played on the team. I got to be the "Bat Girl" for the team. They even got a shirt embroidered for me and my job was to run out and pick up the bats after players threw them down during a play. I would make sure the appropriate bats were ready for the next players. I loved that responsibility, and I had fun getting to know all the players on the team.

My uncle Roy joined the Army, and he was stationed in Germany. At one point, he went AWOL and he showed up on his parents' doorstep one night. I think everyone was surprised by the changed man he'd become. Looking back, I have a feeling he was dealing with post-traumatic stress disorder, but unfortunately that wasn't really something people spoke about at the time. After he returned home, he drank a lot and thanks to his special talent for finding trouble, he was thrown in jail several times. I remember the tension between my grandparents about how to deal with his predicaments. Maw-Maw wanted to bail her son out and give him some extra cash when he needed it. She couldn't stand the thought of one of her kids in need. Paw-Paw felt that his son needed to learn from his mistakes, so he didn't want to bail him out and give him money every time he made a bad decision.

I often accompanied my grandparents when they searched for him, never knowing what we would see when we found him, though normally he was passed out in a friend's apartment somewhere. I'm not sure how they tracked him down – there were no cell phones or GPS at the time – but I guess parental intuition is a powerful thing. He would yell at us as we loaded him in the car and brought him back home again.

I loved my uncle. He was good to me, at least in the way that he liked to encourage me to stay up late and watch movies with him like *Fast Times at Ridgemont High*. He also thought it was funny to make me call bars and ask for "Mike Hunt," only to hear a loud group of people laughing on the other line. I didn't get it. Was his friend Mike not there? What was so funny? It was only years later that I looked back on those memories and realized the real purpose of those prank calls.

One Friday night, when I was about ten and he was particularly bored, he convinced me to hop in his car and go shoot some fireworks off with him. I was rarely comfortable with the things he wanted me to do, but since he was often the only one watching me, I didn't have much of a choice.

It was after eight or nine o'clock that night when we headed off to some distant country road outside San Antonio because he thought it would be funny to light fireworks and shoot them at the cows that were grazing nearby. Once he found a location that suited him, he set a bottle rocket between two rocks and told me I had to light it. I didn't want to and resisted for a while, until I realized we weren't leaving until I complied with his wishes.

I struggled with the lighter, finally lit the wick and whoosh, the rocket took off. It didn't go very high, more like straight out in front of us. He started laughing and I was mortified to see the cows running away, worried that one of them might have been hit.

As we walked back to the car, I didn't immediately notice the faint glow in the distance until my uncle yelled, "Oh shit! We gotta get outta here. The cops'll be here any minute!"

We hopped in the car and sped off, and I watched out of the window as the blaze grew in the distance. When we got home, he insisted that I stay up and watch the late news with him. I was terrified, and he picked up on my anxiety. He kept saying things like, "The police are probably already on the way!"

Then the news came on, and I could hardly believe my eyes. The top story was a fire that had been started on some farmland and had spread over a couple of acres already. I was instantly sick to my stomach, and I lived in total fear for the next several months. Looking back on it now, I'm not sure if it was a coincidence or if that really was the result of what we'd done. In my mind, though, it was all my fault, and I was terrified of the consequences. I think the heavy burden of those childhood experiences made me feel like it was my job to be the serious one and take responsibility for myself and others. I began to realize that I couldn't fully count on anyone but myself, and I was thrust into the care-taker role without even knowing it, and that shaped my decisions for years to come.

Paw-Paw was the one adult I felt could handle the minefield of family challenges that were hovering around us. He managed a paint store and coached softball, and everyone who met him loved him. He was a nice guy who was always willing to lend a hand and make people laugh. The times we had together when I lived there were some of the best times of my life. I loved Maw-Maw dearly, too. Generous and loving, she was the person I spent the most time with when I lived with them because Paw-Paw was normally at work, and Uncle Roy was typically out getting into trouble. She and I would go to farms and pick bushels of strawberries and tomatoes, then we would go home and can endless jars of them. We had great times together.

Although we enjoyed these moments together, Maw-Maw was also a very nervous person. She couldn't relax easily and she almost always stayed home, worrying about one thing or another. I understood her plight without talking about things because I had also become a full-time worrier. After Dad left, I had developed a fear of abandonment, and I picked up the weight of feeling responsible for the rest of the people in the family. I think my deepest fear was that something would happen to one of them that would take them away, and I couldn't bear the thought of that happening again.

Maw-Maw often told me to go outside and find some friends to play with. I couldn't help feeling that she didn't want to be bothered with me in the house, and it was clear that I was to stay outside until dinner, then get to bed. One day, I walked back into the house and found Maw-Maw lying on the floor, unresponsive. I called Paw-Paw at work, and he seemed irritated. He had to leave the paint shop to come home, but he was home in less than thirty minutes. I wasn't sure what was wrong, but he picked her up and she tried to say something, but it was hard to decipher because she was slurring pretty badly.

He put her into her bed, and all he said was "She'll be fine tomorrow." And that was that.

I was teased in school the first couple years after we moved back to San Antonio. Some of the kids at school would yell "redneck" when they saw me get out of my grandparents' car in the mornings. Others called me "gay" because I wasn't interested in boys yet. I spent many hours contemplating my identity at night, wondering "Am I a redneck? Am I gay?" I didn't really have the answers to those questions yet, so I didn't know how to defend myself from the bullying that was happening at school.

Staying at my grandparents' house felt like exploring life without boundaries. I often rode my ten-speed bike for hours to other neighborhoods to meet up with my friends. On one hand, it felt really liberating to explore the world around me so freely. On the other hand, I was a little sad sometimes that nobody seemed to know where I was. Mostly, I enjoyed the freedom that lifestyle afforded me.

(Left): Maw-Maw & Paw-Paw 1970's. (Right): Me and Mom, early 80's.

Trust thyself: every heart vibrates to that iron string. ~Ralph Waldo Emerson

Unbound

Mom dated often in the years after her divorce and I sometimes grew attached, but it seemed that the men I cared about came and went with the wind. Mom was beautiful, and she had a magnetic personality. People loved being around her. Her laugh was so loud and genuine, and she made people feel like they were the only ones in the room.

One day she introduced me to a man named John, and I could tell from the moment I met him that he was going to be around for a while. He really seemed to care about meeting me and making a good impression. They were married within a year, and the three of us moved into a townhouse together. It was the nicest place Mom and I had ever lived in, and I began to feel hope about the future for the first time. They went on a honeymoon to Cozumel, and a couple months after they got back, Mom took me to get my hair cut, and in the car on the way home, she told me that I was going to have a brother. He would be the first Grandson in the family. I was excited for his arrival, but he would be 13 years younger than me, so I wasn't sure what to expect. I had several cousins who were all girls, and we had a great time together. They were like sisters to me.

When my brother was born, there was so much joy floating around. My Grandparents often came over, and I had warm feelings mounting that we finally made it in life. We had a comfortable home, Mom was married, I was staying in the same school instead of moving to a new school every year, and now we had a new baby in the family to fawn over.

One weekend, I stayed the night at my friend Becky's house who lived across the street from my Grandparents. I was thirteen, and I was beginning to explore my independence. We climbed trees in her backyard then walked around to the front yard and Paw-Paw was outside, mowing his front yard across the street.

"Come over and hang out with me for a while" he said.

"We're busy Paw-Paw. Maybe tomorrow. We're going inside to make some dinner". We went inside, and my friend showed me how to make ramen soup on our own, then we watched a movie and had popcorn and went to sleep. The next thing I remember was being shaken awake by Mom at about 5:00 am, and she was obviously distressed.

She said "You need to get dressed and come outside because Paw-Paw is dead."

She didn't have the gift of subtlety, but then again, neither did I. I felt denial, anger, confusion and fear all at once. Paw-Paw wasn't only like a father to me, he was my very best friend in the world. We walked outside my friend's front door, and the first thing I saw was Paw-Paw lying still on a stretcher with unkempt hair, and several police cars and ambulances in the cul-de-sac. *This was really happening.*

The paramedics then loaded him into an ambulance, and we sped behind them to the hospital. They tried for what felt like hours to resuscitate him, and finally a doctor walked into the waiting room where Mom, my Aunt and Uncles, Maw-Maw and I were sitting in silence. It felt like an eternity before he spoke.

"I'm sorry" was all that he said. They asked if we wanted to see him, and somehow I thought that was a good idea. His rustled hair and cold, bluish skin will forever be seared into my memory. I wish I could un-see him like that somehow, and I really wish I could go back in time and hang out with my Paw-Paw the night before.

Maybe if I had stayed with him, he wouldn't have had a heart attack. It felt like it was all my fault that he was gone.

I was gutted. I tried to keep it together at his funeral, but I was a sobbing, inconsolable mess. All of our relatives kept trying to console me. One person I didn't know very well walked up to me and said:

"I remember Willard told me about that time that you two stayed in the cabin, and you made him canned tomato soup, and he said it was the best soup he ever had in his life because you made it."

Really? That's supposed to make me feel better? It isn't working. It's only making this harder. Those were the thoughts that raced through my mind as I tried to regain my composure to make everyone else feel more comfortable. I know they meant well, but the pain of his loss was just too much for me to bear.

My pillar of strength and stability and the person who always knew how to make me laugh was gone. Just like that, without warning. I couldn't make sense of his vanishing, so I had nightmares for the next several years that he was hiding out in other parts of the country not wanting to be found, and somehow I would always find him. It was such a painful time in my life.

For the next five years, things were fairly stable in our home. I babysat my brother a lot, and I played tennis for my school and later tried out for the dance team. Those were good times, and I felt the heavy weight of worry and grief from my childhood lifting. I had some great friends at Judson High School, and we did everything together. We would go to each other's houses to practice for dance, sports, and cheerleading, and we stayed at each other's houses on the weekends. I looked up to my amazing teachers as role models and mentors, and I truly felt surrounded by a village of people who cared about me.

I took my driving test and eventually got my driver's license. I was working part time in the evenings at the local Driving School. One day after work, Mom met me at the door, and I walked out to see a brand new red Hyundai with a huge red bow on top of it sitting in the parking lot. I broke down in tears and fell to my knees. I was in total shock and disbelief.

"No way! Thank you so much! I can't believe it!" I repeated over and over. I hugged Mom and John several times and felt so excited for the generous symbol of freedom and vote of confidence they'd given me that day.

Mom was really strict and protective of me when I became a teenager. I think she felt if she could control my every step, I wouldn't end up in the situation she found herself in at my age. She never told me that, but I assumed as much through the overly strict rules and lack of trust that permeated our relationship. I had so much compassion for her raising a daughter on her own for all of those years, but her rules and consequences were frustrating at the time. I didn't have sex in high school. I didn't do drugs. I went to parties and drank with my friends sometimes, but I did well in school and didn't get into much trouble. If I was five minutes late coming home, there would be hell to pay. I had a hard time understanding it as an audacious teenager. Over time, I really grew to appreciate my Mom for being so stern, but it took a long time for me to fully understand and appreciate it.

Mom often struggled with mood swings. She would be in a great mood one day, then she might spend the next three days in bed not going to work or talking to anyone. There were times that the world just felt like more than she could handle. The hardest part for me was that she had a hard time believing that anyone really loved her. It wasn't until graduate school that I learned from my psychology studies that Mom had most likely been grappling with a mental illness like Bipolar or Borderline Personality Disorder, and my compassion grew enormously as I tried to imagine how difficult that struggle must have been for her. I didn't have the knowledge to understand any of that when I was living at home, but I always guessed that she was struggling with an illness of some kind. I spent countless hours trying to convince her to get therapy, but she made it very clear that she wasn't interested. I think the stigma around mental illness made her feel too intimidated to get the help she needed, and that broke my heart.

The friends that I made in Junior High and High School helped me cope with some of the challenges that I faced at home, like when Paw-Paw passed away or when Mom was going through her mood swings. My friendships provided me the little escape that I occasionally needed to take my mind off things. My best friend Janette was like a sister to me, and I stayed at her house fairly often. Janette was everything I wasn't. She was a cheerleader with porcelain skin and thick, long, curly black hair and the most genuine laugh. She could make me laugh without even trying. She had a very stable, loving family, and they helped to keep me grounded during challenging times.

I had a couple boyfriends during high school, but they never developed into anything too serious because I was completely afraid of commitment. I was worried that if I let myself fall too hard, I would end up getting married or having kids at a young age like Mom. I witnessed every moment of struggle Mom had to endure as a single mother, and I knew I wasn't prepared to take on those challenges. I had dreams of going to college and building a career for myself so I never had to rely on anyone else for anything I needed.

During the second half of my junior year, the economy was in freefall, and John had been laid off from his job. At the time, I had a routine where I gave a friend a ride to and from school each day. One day, we walked around the parking lot several times looking for my car before finally coming to the grave conclusion that my car had been stolen. We told all of our friends, and we even went to the school administration office to file a report.

It wasn't until a while later that I heard from Pam that my car had been repossessed. Apparently, my dad stopped paying child support payments, and Mom and John were short on money and couldn't afford to keep up with the monthly car payments. The collection agency warned them that they would be repossessing the car, but I think they were just too embarrassed to tell me about it, so that is how I found out. I had never expected them to get me a car. As a matter of fact, I was working at the Driving School so I could save my own money towards a car. I was profoundly grateful to them for the generous gift, but I felt guilty that it had become a burden for them, and I would have happily contributed to the cost of it had I known what was going on behind the scenes. It was embarrassing to admit to my friends what really happened to my car that day, and I began to wonder if things were okay at home.

A few weeks before my senior year of high school, Mom and John told me that they would be moving from San Antonio to Austin. It wasn't up for discussion and it was happening in a couple of weeks. They needed to move for work and financial reasons.

I'd formed such strong bonds with my friends over the years, and I had several extra-curricular commitments I had made with my school. I was desperately looking forward to spending my final year of high school with my best friends. I was on the dance team at school, and we had been practicing all summer for our upcoming performances. I took my commitments to my teammates seriously, and all of our routines were choreographed based upon the number of people on our team. I couldn't imagine suddenly abandoning my responsibilities and friends to move to an entirely new city where I wouldn't know a soul.

When they gave me this news, the first thing I thought was that I wished my dad lived closer. He never seemed to be around when I needed him. I asked Mom and John if there was any way I could stay in San Antonio and live with my aunt Pam and her daughter, Kim. I had been close to Pam since I was little, and Kim was like a little sister to me. I would sometimes stay over at her house on the weekends. Pam was all for it, and they finally came to an agreement allowing me to live with her. It made for a unique senior year because my mom, step-dad and brother weren't there with me, but it was the best option available to us under the circumstances.

I was excited to live with Pam because she was so much fun to be around. She loved to take me to baseball games and the mall with her. She had a youthful personality and similar facial features to my mom so it felt like home being around her. For a while, the routine worked pretty well, and we had fun. Eventually though, disagreements and discrepancies grew between Mom and Pam about expenses that weren't being paid as agreed upon because my parents were short on money. That created more tension around the house so I began to feel like I was a burden and caught in the middle of it all. I called Mom to explain that to her, telling her I just didn't feel right staying there any longer. She was very compassionate.

She assured me by saying "We'll come down tonight and figure things out. Don't worry, Baby."

She and John drove to Pam's that night to help me get my things together, and Janette and her family generously agreed to let me stay with them for the remainder of the school year.

When Mom arrived, she came inside and told Pam the plan and that we needed to get my things, but Pam refused because she wanted me to stay. They got into a huge argument that turned physical as I watched, paralyzed in horror. They were wrestling around on the ground, pulling the phone out of the wall by the cord at one point. While John sat outside in the car, I stood by, watching the whole thing, silent, baffled. I didn't want to take sides, and I could tell that years' worth of anger and frustration were culminating in that moment.

Finally, I yelled out, "Stop, you guys! Let's just leave and figure this out later."

I ran outside and asked John to come in and help me get them to stop. Eventually, they separated and we left. They both survived with scratches and bruises, but it was very traumatic for all of us and our hearts were so heavy as we drove to a hotel that night. I felt so badly that Mom and Pam got into such a big fight that night. It really sunk in that everything was my fault. My senior year wasn't going as I envisioned, and I was beginning to feel as though I should have just moved to Austin with my family and started over. Mom dropped me off at Janette's house at the end of the weekend; and I felt a tangled web of gratitude, guilt, and shame for putting that burden on their family.

The following Monday morning at school, this announcement came over the intercom:

"Rachel Fredholm, please come to the principal's office." My face turned beet-red. Mr. Parsley, our principal, was the sweetest man and a great leader for our school. He was such a champion for the students, and he was my good friend Lisa's uncle. I trusted him completely. Even so, this couldn't be good.

"Hi, Mr. Parsley. I heard you wanted to see me?" I said nervously.

"Sit down, Rachel. I heard what's going on at home."

I was mortified, but I felt comforted at the same time that I had someone I could talk to who might be able to help. I explained that I still needed to get my belongings from Aunt Pam's, but he said he didn't think it was a good idea for me to go unaccompanied – he'd heard about the fight. Clueless as to how he knew, I was grateful for his help.

He picked up the phone and called a police officer to escort me to Pam's house. I was so humiliated and scared to arrive at my aunt's house in a cop car – it seemed so dramatic and unnecessary. Pam had told us she was changing the lock to the door, though, and with Mom and John back in Austin, I didn't know what else to do.

The officer was very polite and walked with me up to the house. We were hoping she would be at work and I could use my key but when we knocked she was home and told us through the closed door that she didn't have to work that day. He asked if I could please come in and get my things and she let us in.

I was so uncomfortable. I wanted to talk to Pam and explain that she didn't do anything to me. I was just caught in the middle and didn't want the situation to cause any more friction between her and Mom. I was sad about what transpired and disappointed over how things ended, but I simply couldn't find the right words. She didn't speak to me either as I picked up my belongings with the officer watching over us. I put my things into the trunk of the cop car and he drove me to Janette's house so I could take my things inside – I'd been excused from school for the rest of the day. It wasn't until years later that I realized Mom must have been the one who called the principal that day to request his help coordinating the collection of my belongings.

For the rest of that year I felt like such an outsider in my own life. I didn't have a home with my own family, and I was overly aware and hypersensitive to the burden I had become. No one ever complained or said anything like that to me, but I felt like a misfit and a loser deep inside my bones. I didn't invite friends over after school because I was keenly aware it wasn't my house. I lost the confidence I worked so hard to build that year, too. I began to feel like a drifter that didn't belong anywhere. My grades dropped a bit that year, and depression crept in. I tried to hold my feelings inside, but it was obvious that I wasn't myself.

In my English class, we read the essay "Self-Reliance" by Ralph Waldo Emerson, and the words sank like weights to a dark corner of my heart, and they've been with me ever since. That essay helped me to believe, for the first time, that the choices I made could actually impact the trajectory of my life. I was still too young to understand the true power of those words or how to put them into action. But, until that moment, I truly believed I was destined to live the life I was born into, and I didn't think there was anything I could do to influence my own outcome.

Finally, the end of the school year arrived, and I still felt lost and unsure what my next move was going to be. It was so hard to imagine my friends and I going our separate ways but it was inevitable. Eventually, I decided to go to an affordable state college in North Texas since I needed to work to pay for my education and didn't want to be a burden on anyone. I had received partial academic scholarships to a few out of state schools, but the remaining tuition was still way more than I could afford. I got the feeling that my family would be happier if I didn't go to college at all. It was going to be a big expense, and it took me away from home so they wouldn't be able to keep close tabs on me. But I was determined to make a better life for myself, and nothing was going to hold me back.

I was excited to live in the campus dorm my freshman year. It was the first time I got to make decisions for myself each day, and I was definitely ready to have that freedom. I felt lonely sometimes without my family and a posse of lifelong friends nearby, and I didn't have student council and dance team to help define my identity. I felt a bit lost that year like an untethered boat drifting at sea.

I began to wonder if the independence I'd been craving for so long was really all it was cracked up to be. I had no idea what I wanted to do with my life, and I couldn't clearly identify my passions. I was lost and needed that learning experience, but I didn't really feel like my life had any purpose. I went to class and made good grades, but I also enjoyed going to parties with my friends. I didn't go out that often, but when I did, I struggled with knowing when to stop drinking. Alcohol abuse has been a silent struggle in my family. I'm genetically predisposed to have the same problems, so I have to be vigilant. When I first got my taste of freedom, I did what so many college kids do- I pushed my limits. It never got out of hand, and I didn't get into any trouble, but it was a lesson I had to learn through trial and error. Thankfully after I left graduate school and learned to become a responsible, working adult, I matured and became much more capable of making better decisions for myself. I'm relieved that I don't really enjoy drinking in the same way I did when I was younger. I was clearly trying to fill a void and cover up feelings of low self-esteem and lack of purpose. If I could go back in time and say anything to that lost, assailable version of myself, I would say: "Find your passions. You are worthy."

My dad re-entered my life after I moved away from home and offered to help me a little with some of my school and living expenses. He still lived in Europe, but he called and wrote and made occasional visits to see me. He showed me how to make a monthly budget for my expenses, and to this day those gestures have made such a tremendous difference to the outcome of my life. I'll always be grateful to him for it.

That year I met my first true love, David. He was handsome and smart, and he enjoyed books and music – two of my favorite things. I was deeply enamoured but it was young love, and we had our whole lives ahead of us. I transferred to the University of Texas at Austin my sophomore year, and we decided not to hold each other back from important life experiences with the burden of a long-distance relationship. In retrospect, I think my low self-esteem at the time may have opened the door to self-sabotage. I didn't feel worthy of asking someone that I loved to make important sacrifices for me.

In high school, I'd dreamed of being a sports or news broadcaster but my family's struggles inspired me to learn more about psychology. I was so hopeful that I would learn something that could help prevent those struggles from being passed down to me and future generations. Unfortunately, I didn't take college that seriously, studying just enough to get the grades I needed. I felt lost and unmotivated through the experience, and I didn't retain much of what I learned. There was a lack of accountability in the giant classrooms of a thousand students. I crammed before exams and a week later that information was no longer accessible in my brain. I studied psychology but I had no idea what I wanted to do once I graduated. I was hoping to heal the cycle of troubles that haunted my family, but I had no idea how to apply what I was learning to the real world and earn a living.

I made the most of living in a city known for being the "live music capitol of the world." On any given night there were a quiver of live music options, and I enjoyed the escape that it provided me. In those moments, all my cares were gone. If I couldn't find an actual person who could relate to my particular worries, I could find a companion through music. I scrounged together the tip money I earned at work to go and see any live music I could. One night I would be dancing to a ska band in an abandoned garage, the next I would end up in a friend's backyard listening to a little-known bluegrass band.

I made some great friends while I was in college, but Tara and Jules were my besties. Tara had dark brown hair and brown eyes, and she was the yin to my yang. She was very sensible but always up for an adventure. She was on a clear path in school, and she knew that she wanted to pursue work in accounting. I was the polar opposite. I was getting a liberal arts degree in psychology, but I was completely lost and unsure about what I wanted to do with my degree. We balanced each other out pretty well and enjoyed listening to live music, dancing, and ski trips that provided a release from school and work. I got a full-time job waiting tables at a restaurant to pay my rent and bills.

Jules was one of the first friends I made at the restaurant. She had curly, strawberry blonde hair, and she was always the life of the party. We were in the same psychology classes at UT, and we were roommates for a while. She would often bring home groups of friends from her sorority or the UT baseball team. People gravitated towards her, and she was great at making people laugh with the best jokes. I soon realized that I was not quite as extroverted as I once thought, noticing I needed quiet nights at home to help me recharge my batteries. I wasn't capable of being a social butterfly in the same way as Jules, but I really enjoyed her positive energy. She helped to pull me out of my shell and introduce me to new people. In my free time I volunteered for several psychology professors, working on research and grant projects. The next logical step, it seemed, was to apply to graduate school – that's what my research cohorts were doing. Without giving it much thought, I took the GRE and applied to PhD programs in Industrial/Organizational Psychology. Dad flew in from Europe to take a trip with me through the northeastern US where we visited several graduate school programs.

That trip meant so much to me because I could tell he valued my desire to get a higher education, and he made the time to help me explore my options. If he hadn't made that trip a priority to help me visit those schools, I'm not sure I would have pursued a graduate degree. I will be forever grateful to him for that trip together. George Washington University was my first choice, and I was wait-listed but didn't get in. I really liked the laid-back vibe of the small town of Blacksburg so eventually I accepted an offer to enter the PhD program at Virginia Tech.

The only thing holding me back was the guilt, that felt like a cargo ship, weighing on my shoulders. I'd spent my life, up to that point, trying to help my family navigate their problems.

If I move away, who will be there to help them with their next crisis? I worried.

Through my undergraduate studies in Psychology, I learned that I could not control or change my family's problems, and the best thing I could do was to focus on taking control of my own life. I actually consulted a therapist about this decision, and she advised me that I was not responsible for my family's problems or their happiness, and that the only thing I could control was my own outcome. She helped me release my feelings of guilt and realize that by choosing to continue my education, I wasn't abandoning my family. More importantly, I wasn't abandoning myself. So, I moved to Virginia and enrolled in the PhD program. I did my best to write letters and talk on the phone to my family and come back for visits whenever I could afford it.

Aunt Pam (Left) Mom (Right) Mid 1980's

The greatest glory in living lies not in never falling, but in rising every time we fall.
~Nelson Mandela

Lemonade

In graduate school, I spent a lot of time with a group of friends who were in the same graduate program. We met each other's families and took road trips together. At some point we developed a game where each person in the group was represented by the head or tail of a coin. For example, Trina would be Quarter Heads or Tim would be Penny Tails. Each person had a handful of coins and we would go around the circle, presenting a scenario like, "This person would be most likely to rob a bank." Then each of us would choose from our pile of coins the one that represented the person we thought best matched the scenario. We played this game often and it always brought lots of laughter and reflection. It was so eye-opening to have everyone pull their hands away to see who received a majority vote for each scenario.

One winter, our group went on a ski trip and we played this game. Someone said, "This person is most likely to go into a different profession." I vividly remember everyone pulling their hands away, and all the coins on the table cast a vote for me.

Was it really that obvious that I wasn't passionate about my studies? I wondered, in disbelief.

It was, but I was the last person to realize it. Once I completed my master's degree, I realized that I wasn't cut out for that field. There was so much pressure to do research and publish articles in academic journals. Apparently, the more articles a graduate program publishes in highly regarded journals, the more funding they receive. Getting an article published in one of the highly regarded journals often requires years' worth of research, and sometimes the articles are published in a mediocre journal that doesn't yield the same level of funding. The part that I struggled with most was the fact that the people who would benefit the most from the results of the research were often the least likely to read it.

Still, I convinced myself for a couple years that I wanted to pursue that path. Eventually, it became apparent to me that the field just didn't light a fire in me. I went in to talk to my graduate advisor, and I was surprised when he told me he noticed that my interest in my studies seemed to wax and wane. Because I had so much respect for him and valued his opinion, our talk that day was like holding a mirror up to my deepest untapped thoughts and insecurities. I was terrified to admit aloud to him that this field wasn't the right fit for me, and I was equally saddened and relieved to find that he already knew it. He gave me the encouragement I needed to pursue a new path and told me that if I found the drive and passion to come back to complete my PhD, I could reach out and let him know. I left his office in tears, unsure of what my future held. I received my master's degree, then I moved on without completing my PhD. Reflecting back on this experience, it appears this may have been another example of self-sabotaging behavior due to low self-esteem. It was easy to blame my lack of commitment on not feeling passionate about the field, but I think it may have had more to do with the fact that I didn't believe in myself or think I was good enough to get my PhD.

Still, my time in the little town of Blacksburg, Virginia, was both memorable and transformational. I felt like a failure at times for not completing my PhD, but I met some truly wonderful people and learned so much about myself during that time. With some distance from home in the rear-view mirror, I began to realize that I had always been such a people-pleaser. I did my best to make everyone else happy but I never stopped to think about what I wanted, needed, or believed. While I was in Blacksburg, I began to unearth my voice. I learned how to stand up for what I believed in even if it wasn't going to make everyone else happy, and that felt really good.

I was determined to find a great job to prove to myself that I didn't need to have a PhD to do work that I enjoyed. I was determined to carve a path for myself that was meaningful and fun. For the first time in my life I could pull out a map and go anywhere my heart desired, and I was excited by all the possibilities. Somehow, I knew intuitively that I was going to San Francisco, though I had no solid reason to justify that choice. I didn't have any family or friends in San Francisco and I had never been there. What drew me there was the idea of being surrounded by free-thinking people. I felt like those were my people, even though I didn't know a soul in that city. Maybe, I hoped, for the first time in my life, I would fit in somewhere.

I moved to San Francisco and shortly thereafter my boyfriend (another David) and I had a long talk and decided to break up. He was still in Virginia pursuing a dual master's in engineering and architecture, and he was also a musician and artist. We dated for a couple years during graduate school, but he was really serious and worked long hours on his schoolwork, pottery, and music. He was a kind and hugely talented person, but being with him always seemed to highlight my own shortcomings and made me feel like I should have been making more of myself somehow. My heartbreak was quickly soothed by the immediate connection I felt with my new surroundings, and it was almost as though the city itself filled the void of that relationship. It felt great to be single and explore my new stomping grounds without anything holding me back.

I always dreamed of living in San Francisco, and it did not disappoint. Because the parking challenges and expenses made it so prohibitive to have a car in the city, I sold my Jeep when I moved there and spent the next five years without a car, either walking or taking the bus everywhere I went. It was a great way to explore the city, getting lost in the alleys and side streets. There was always something new to discover – art, music, architecture, people, books. I was intoxicated by the sensory overload of it all. I was living fully in the moment for the first time in my life, and it felt so liberating.

I got a job working as a Selection & Development Specialist at an online wine company during the dot-com boom. We received massages and had wine and cheese tastings during the work day. And we enjoyed elaborate dinners and had private concerts at vineyards in Napa on the weekends. There was a rampant feeling of hedonism flowing through the streets of the city during those years of the dot-com bubble. It was an exciting time to be living and working in the city, but it felt as though the start-up companies were also swept up in the moment, not giving much thought to the future.

I had become good friends with a girl who lived nearby (an aspiring singer named Sam), as well as three guys (two were architects and one was a financial analyst). Somehow, we all agreed that we would call ourselves "Pente," and we were inseparable. They all seemed to be chasing their dreams, yet I was still unsure what I wanted to do with my life. I hadn't found my path yet, but I was having fun and being truly light-hearted for the first time in my life.

I had a passion for photography so I offered to take some black-and-white photos of Sam on my roof for her new demo CD. I loved the look of the gravel and textured walls on my roof and the view of the Golden Gate Bridge from there was arresting. It was the first time I played around with something I was passionate about outside of work. I'd recently bought a nice camera, and I was having fun experimenting with it. I deeply appreciated the magic of those moments where I felt the freedom to tap into my passions and live in the moment.

Something about the combined interests and curiosity that we shared as a group made Pente an interesting social dynamic. We made elaborate meals together and played chess. We went to music festivals where we camped and sat around campfires with legendary musicians while they casually jammed together. We indulged in bone marrow, drank fantastic wine, explored remote surfing beaches, painted collaborative paintings in Golden Gate Park, and played guitar together on the roof of my studio apartment, where I slept each night in the closet so that I could pretend I had an actual bedroom that was separate from my tiny living room space. We went to art openings and explored every inch of the city together on foot, doing our best to convince ourselves that we had no romantic interest in each other so that we could prolong the dynamic of the friendships.

One time, a few of us had the unique opportunity to house-sit for a well-known wine importer and author, and I tried on his wife's thigh-high velvet boots while we listened to Bob Dylan as we drank delicious wine. The opulent dining room we enjoyed fantastic meals in reminded me of a scene from *The Shining*. Everyone sat around the garden in the morning playing guitar and singing. I felt as though I had found a place where I could be myself and belonged for the first time. I was trying to squeeze every ounce of fun out of my weekends to blow off some steam from the grueling hours I was putting in at my job during the week.

I rode the MUNI bus to and from work and as I was on my way home from work late one night, I was staring at my paycheck for the entire hour-long ride back to my tiny studio apartment. There were five figures on my paycheck, and that was for just two weeks of work. I had a hard time believing that a young woman like me who rode the bus to and from work each day was making this much money despite the fact that I was working just as hard as my peers who were earning the same amount.

Just a couple years before that I had moved into my studio apartment in San Francisco with no furniture, sleeping on the hardwood floor in my sleeping bag for the first month. My loving, generous mom bought me a bed for Christmas. We crammed it into my closet, and that was where I slept every night for the next few years. I still didn't own a car and slept in a closet, but I was making more money than I deserved — that's how I felt anyway.

I was working really long hours, often arriving at 6am to work and not leaving the office until 9pm. I would even continue to write emails before I went to bed in the evenings and often worked on the weekends, too. I was earning the money I was being paid, but for some reason I didn't feel worthy of it. I felt like it was a mistake or that I'd stolen it somehow.

This poor girl from Texas who came from a broken home was never meant to accomplish anything. That was the story that was still playing in my head, and I struggled with feeling worthy.

Some truly brilliant, creative minds worked together for that company, including Megan and Sarah who became close personal friends. Everyone hoped the company would go public one day and we could all retire together in Central America but that day never came. It was too good to be true; eventually, the bottom dropped out. While the company was making the front covers of magazines and everyone thought the future looked bright, they were burning through money faster than they could raise it and it just wasn't sustainable. We underwent mass layoffs, and I had to do some of the dirty work. I was there until the end and it was a soul-sucking experience to have to layoff friends and co-workers who I really cared about and who had worked insanely long hours toward the same goal for years.

The dot-com bubble finally burst and our company closed its doors. I decided to commiserate with some co-workers in Golden Gate Park, so we met up with forties in brown bags to fully embrace our newfound unemployed status. I was amazed by how full the park was on a weekday. Everyone was communally drinking, smoking weed, playing guitar, and throwing frisbee, seemingly without a care in the world. But I felt the constant undercurrent that loomed below. We were all in need of jobs, and they were in short supply. That carefree lifestyle wouldn't last without a solid income in a city known for its outrageous rental prices. We went back to my friend Megan's house, and her roommate was in his pajamas in the middle of the afternoon, which was oddly common in San Francisco at the time. So many people worked from home or were being laid-off that it was like a big block party that extended across the city.

There wasn't a comparable job to be found in San Francisco as companies were going under left and right. I quickly decided that looking for a job at that time would be pointless and I wanted to do something more meaningful. I was also in pursuit of a healthier lifestyle and a spiritual journey, so I pursued a dream to climb Machu Picchu. I found a mileage ticket to Peru for a month, and three days later I was on a flight to Lima.

Me & Megan, San Francisco, CA

Fearlessness is like a muscle. I know from my own life that the more I exercise it the more natural it becomes to not let my fears run me. ~Arianna Huffington

Inca Trail

When I first arrived in Lima, I began to realize how thoroughly unprepared I was for the trip. I was craving some spontaneity, but I hadn't even arranged for transportation from the airport, and I didn't bring traveler's checks or my cell phone. I spent more than two hours exchanging some US dollars for Peruvian sol, making calls from a pay phone to arrange a hotel for the night, then piecing together the little Spanish I could remember from college to book a shuttle into the city. It quickly became clear to me that I needed to hurry as they kept shouting, "*Vamonos!*" The shuttle was about to leave.

I approached the shuttle cautiously because it was clearly full. Not only were all the seats taken, but people were standing in every open space. I tried to explain that there was no room for me, but they just motioned for me to hold onto the side panel of the shuttle where a door should have been attached. This would not fly in the US. I nervously climbed onboard and held onto the roof of the shuttle with one hand and the back of one of the seats with the other.

As we made our way onto the highway and toward the city center, I was amazed by the traffic, smog, honking, and crazy driving. I had never been in a city like this before. Over eight million people lived in Lima at the time and I was struck by the feeling that this idea was a huge mistake. Fortunately, they dropped me off at my modest hotel for the evening and I found myself in Miraflores.

After I checked in and put my backpack down in my room, I decided to walk around and find some dinner. Two blocks away I made my way into a small, unassuming restaurant and took a seat at the bar, not wanting to take up a table by myself. The bartender helped me with the menu and I ordered some ceviche and a pisco sour. He proceeded to tell me that I needed to try something called "tiger's milk." I never like to turn down a good recommendation, so I agreed.

When he brought my ceviche out, he also handed me the "tiger's milk"- a small shot glass of what appeared to be cloudy, watered-down milk. *Hmm. This felt like another mistake.* I didn't want to offend him by refusing to try it, but I had visions of getting sick on my first night in a new country. I tried to explain my concerns to him, but he very calmly and confidently convinced me that I would love it and I had to try it, so I did. The tangy juice of the ceviche was delicious. Finally, something felt like it was going my way and I decided that it was a good omen for the trip. I walked back to my room and slept hard that night.

I quickly realized that this city was too much for me and made my way out of Lima. I camped in several remote places and took the bus across the country before ending up in Cusco. I knew I wanted to do the hike to Machu Picchu, but I was enjoying my time in Cusco so much that I ended up spending more time there exploring the museums, hiking in the nearby area and getting to know the locals.

Though I'd traveled before to a few countries in Europe to see my dad, and my ex-boyfriend and I backpacked through Europe during graduate school, that was the extent of my travels before I arrived in Peru. I was fascinated by the culture and way of life there. Everything was much simpler and my troubles felt like they were melting away. I arranged to do the hike to Machu Picchu. I met up with a tour company and a few other people who were going to do the hike with me in the lobby of a hotel in Cusco.

The group was a mix of people from Canada, Germany, Australia, and the US. I was paired up with my tent mate, a doctor from Colorado. We spent the next few days doing training hikes around Cusco, then we spent a couple nights on the islands of Amantani and Taquile, sleeping on mats inside mud huts hosted by local families. Then we explored the floating islands of Uros during the day and did more training hikes in the afternoons.

Finally, we were ready to begin our trek to Machu Picchu, one of the world's most iconic archaeological sites. My reasons for wanting to hike the Inca Trail were spiritual. I was at a crossroads, and I was seeking clarity about what I wanted to do with my life.

We opted to do the four-day Classic Inca Trail, which entailed reaching an elevation of 13,829 feet over Dead Woman's Pass, Warmi Wanusca. The pass was grueling for the group as we struggled with altitude sickness. Thankfully, I didn't have a bad case of it, but a couple people had to go back down for a while to catch their breath before they could continue. We experienced the common symptoms of headaches, nausea and shortness of breath, but we just kept putting one foot in front of the other until we made our way over the big pass. On the final morning, we were woken at 3am with coca tea and flashlights. They told us that the most magical way to experience Machu Picchu was to hike to the Sun Gate where we would watch the sun rise over Machu Picchu and this was how we would see it for the first time. It was, without a doubt, one of the most awe-inspiring moments of my life.

Another reason I wanted to hike the Inca Trail, instead of taking the train, was simply because there would be fewer people. They only allow 500 climbers on the mountain per day and 300 of those are porters, which means only 200 tourists are allowed on the various trails to Machu Picchu on any given day. After we explored the ruins that morning, we began the long hike down the mountain. When we finally arrived at the bottom, we explored the little town of Aguas

Calientes and sat in the natural hot springs there. Nobody seemed to mind the murky brown water. We all stunk and had blisters and sore feet, so the waters were soothing for us all.

Next, we took a train to a cabin on the banks of the Amazon River. That was our base for rainforest hikes and nighttime canoe trips down the river where we looked for nocturnal animals along the riverbanks. I did a lot of soul-searching on that trip and decided that I didn't want to work in the corporate world anymore because it felt like a meaningless pursuit of financial gain. I befriended several Peruvians during my trip, and they taught me so much about what really matters in life- love, family, friendship, and pursing your passions. These people I met were deeply happy, but none of them had any money. I was inspired to make a career change as soon as I got back to San Francisco.

On the way home I had a layover in Costa Rica where I met up with Tara. We sat in hot springs together, went ziplining through the jungle, and stayed in what felt like luxurious digs after just returning from a month of tent camping in Peru. I still had modest savings that I'd accumulated from my job in San Francisco, and it felt like a worthwhile splurge after roughing it for so long.

Arriving back in San Francisco was a strong culture shock. It was as though this place I had called home for several years was suddenly foreign to me, and I didn't belong. The bustling streets and crowded restaurants and bars were filled with people wearing high heels and leather jackets and I found myself annoyed by it all. Everything went into slow motion. I was more observant and watched a group of people walk down the street, tripping over a homeless man lying on the sidewalk. They laughed and kept walking, seemingly unaware that a human being lay suffering on the ground. I felt nauseous. It wasn't just their callous behavior that struck me, but the realization that I had lived here for years before my trip to Peru without really noticing those things. I moved into a flat with a group of young professionals, but I felt a bit lost. I had some savings to pay my bills, but there was still a lack of available jobs in Organizational Development during those tumultuous times in Silicon Valley, and I still felt at a crossroads with what I was going to do with my life.

Around that time, I woke up to news of the September 11th terrorist attacks. I called my family and friends, paralyzed with fear about the extent of what could happen. My roommates still had their jobs, but most of them came home early from work that day and we sat together in the living room, finding comfort in companionship during such a frightening moment in time. Alonso and Amber were the roommates I connected with the most, and we were glued to the television, watching in horror as the events of the day unfolded. I couldn't navigate my life or make decisions very well at the time, but I was so stubbornly committed to the idea of abandoning the corporate world that I went about the farthest I possibly could in the other direction. I would have probably been better off if I'd chosen something perhaps a little more in the middle, but instead I decided the next logical step for me in that moment was to become a dog trainer. I passionately loved animals, and I felt like I could trust them more than I could trust people at the time. It wasn't long though, before everything began to smell like poop, and packs of dogs were pulling me around the city.

My thirtieth birthday arrived, and I felt an overwhelming feeling of failure. In the city it seemed like everyone had high-paying corporate jobs, spoke multiple languages, had a start-up business on the side and did triathlons. I was a single, thirty-year-old dog trainer. I was trying to buck the system somehow, but I had this overwhelming feeling that I'd been the one thrown off track. To celebrate my birthday, a group of us drove north of San Francisco to a house in Sea Ranch. We drove over the Golden Gate Bridge, which had been threatened after the 9/11 attacks, but we all made a choice not to live our lives in fear. My friends thoughtfully arranged for us to enjoy oysters at sunset and jump rope with kelp from the beach and we had a fantastic seafood dinner with stellar wine. Afterwards, they came walking toward me together in silence. *Wait a minute. Were they really wearing my clothes?* Each person was also wearing a printed mask of my face with different expressions. It was really creepy and it scared the living shit out of me, but it was really thoughtful, too. Suddenly, I didn't feel like such a failure because I had such wonderful friends.

Machu Picchu, Peru.

(Left): Ziplining w/ Tara in Costa Rica. (Right): My friends wearing creepy face masks

The entire universe conspired to help me find you. ~Paulo Coelho

First Sight

My trip to Peru gave me a new perspective. I knew what it felt like to be inspired, and I realized that I wanted to do something more meaningful with my time. So, I signed up to do several volunteer projects. I knew that if I was doing work that helped others, I would find more peace and eventually find my path forward. One of the projects was a three-day breast cancer walk where participants walk twenty miles per day for three days and camp overnight. A good friend of mine lost her mom to breast cancer, so I wanted to support her and was excited to spend a long weekend with inspirational women. My volunteer role required that I drive a moving truck from one location to the next with all the signs needed to set up camp each day. Our team would unload all the signs and place them around camp, then break them down the next morning and set them up at the next site.

I was thoroughly enjoying the event as I met dozens of breast cancer survivors and did my small part to organize the signage for the event. At the end of each day, there were inspirational talks given by breast cancer survivors and I felt like what I was doing really mattered. We worked long hours each day until almost midnight, but it was so much fun and so inspiring. Time flew by so quickly each day and I didn't want it to end.

While we were unloading the large wind master signs from the back of the truck, I looked over my shoulder and caught a glimpse of the most gorgeous human I had ever laid eyes on. This young guy was wearing a straw hat and no shirt and his tanned, muscular body was a sight to behold. He was driving a giant forklift and that made him seem even more manly and interesting to me. Although men don't normally catch my eye in a physical way, something very primal kept pulling my attention his way.

That night, after I wrapped up work with my team, I laid my sleeping bag down in the back of my truck. It was late and lacking the energy to set up my tent that day, I decided to sleep in the back of the truck because we had to meet back there at 5a.m. to work the event.

Realizing I didn't have an alarm clock with me (this was before smartphones were around), I was worried that I wouldn't wake up on time. I looked up to see if anyone else was around who could wake me up in the morning. At that very moment, the handsome forklift guy walked right out of the dense fog in front of my truck. Taking this as fate, I asked him if anyone on their team would be awake by five and, if so, could someone please knock on the back of the truck to make sure I was up? He said that he had to be awake early in the morning and he would wake me up.

Somehow, in the span of about five minutes, we managed to talk about photography, travel, and dogs. It turned out that these were a few of his favorite things too.

Hmm. Where's the catch? I wondered.

He probably didn't like women, or maybe he had a girlfriend. I had no idea where he lived or whether he would actually wake me up in the morning. I thought there was a good chance I would never see him again. I crawled into my sleeping bag and fell fast asleep.

The next morning, I woke up to a knock on the back of the truck. I startled awake with my nappy hair and puffy eyes to find the tall forklift guy standing behind the truck.

"Hey, I just wanted to make sure you were awake."

Wow, this gorgeous man also knew how to keep a promise to help a stranger. "Thanks. I'm glad you remembered." I said, a little too eagerly.

He explained that his name was Matt, and he worked for the production company that organized these events and he traveled from one city to the next with a crew of amazing people who became close friends. After they were finished with the San Francisco event that night, they would leave for New York City the next day. *Okay, there was the catch.*

After all the walkers made their way to Chrissy Field, under the backdrop of the Golden Gate Bridge, we were told to return the equipment for the event. As luck would have it, Matt was standing next to the truck where I had to return my gear.

We chatted for just a few minutes and loosely agreed to get together after the event with some of our friends. We exchanged numbers. Over the course of the three or four minutes we were talking, two women called over the radios to tell Matt to get back to work. We were being watched, and I could tell there were some women who were very protective over this guy. On that note, I told him I needed to head out. I could tell he was embarrassed about the radio calls, but I didn't want to step on anyone's toes.

I joined my volunteer crew and we walked over to the event's closing ceremonies. We listened to a variety of speakers and survivors speak about their experiences with breast cancer and they shared a determination to rid the planet of this awful disease. It was a beautiful, blue bird day overlooking a city that I loved and I was so inspired by it all.

I went home feeling so moved by the incredible women I met, speeches I heard and acts of kindness I witnessed over that long weekend, but I also felt a different kind of inspiration. I thought it was interesting that I met an amazing man after I signed up to do meaningful volunteer work that inspired me.

When I got home, one of my roommates told me he caught a salmon that day on a boat trip and offered to share it with the rest of us. I invited some friends over too and we made fantastic sushi. It was a great evening. Still, I kept thinking about the inspirational people I had met that weekend and I was swept up with thoughts about how much more I could be making of my life. As the night grew later, I remembered that Matt and I talked about meeting up with our friends, but I didn't have the courage to call him.

That was such a fluke, I thought. *I'm sure he and his team have to work late, and they are leaving for New York early tomorrow.*

Just about the time that this realization came over me, my phone rang. *It was him!* He wanted to know if I wanted to meet him and his friends at their hotel for some drinks. It was already after nine, and I had to work the next day. I forgot to mention to him earlier that I didn't have a car. I told him that I was sorry, but I couldn't make it out to see him and my friends were about to leave to go home, too. I thought for sure we would never see each other or speak again.

"What if I come to your place?" he offered, surprising me. I knew he probably didn't have a car either. "I can just take a taxi over," he added.

Was this really happening?

Completely shocked, I nervously replied, "Okay," texted him my address, then begged my friends to stay until he got there because I was nervous to be alone with him this late at night.

They apologized and said they really had to get going because we all had work the next day. I promised to text them if anything was strange or suspicious at all.

A little later, around 10pm, there was a light knock on the front door. I nervously answered it and Matt was standing there, shyly, carrying a small, black duffel bag. *Wait … what?* My mind raced.

"What's in the duffel bag?" I asked, picturing a knife or maybe a rope and chopped-up body parts.

"Photo albums" he said innocently.

"Are you kidding me?! You really scared me for a minute!" We sat out there talking about the contents of the duffel bag for several minutes before I invited him inside.

I made him a gin and tonic and put on some music, and we looked through his pictures and talked for hours. I was completely swept off my feet. He was so sweet and unassuming. I began to wonder if he was really interested in me in a romantic way because he hadn't tried to kiss me … until a quiet moment came, and the sparks flew.

I was relieved he was okay with taking things slowly. I really wanted to get to know him better and if the stars aligned the way I hoped, there would be more opportunities for us to be together. He stayed the night and the next morning I did something I had never done for a man before. I called in sick, deciding to spend the morning with Matt. We took the bus to a nude beach nearby and we played in the sand and water as old naked men surfed over our heads. I guess I thought that he should get to know the real me and the crazy adventures I always found myself chasing. If he wasn't down with this scenario, then we would never be a match. I could tell that I'd found a kindred spirit. He was all about it: The bus. The naked old men surfing over us. The spontaneity of it all. We clearly inspired each other, and I felt sure in my heart we would see each other again one day. I just had no idea when.

A couple months later, Matt told me that he had to make a trip to Oregon, and he was wondering if I wanted to meet up with him there for a little road trip. At first, I hesitated because I realized I was a few years older than him, and his job entailed traveling around the country. I wasn't sure it all made sense.

When I mentioned my doubts about our age difference, he said "Girl, you're barely mature enough for me." I spit out my water, laughing at his reply. *Touche.*

We set off on our road trip through Oregon. When we reached the coast, we were prepared to camp in the rain because that region isn't known for its sunshine. We stopped at a tiny shop and bought some oysters then hiked down to the ocean in Seaside with our tent and sleeping bags slung over our backs. We were stunned to be greeted by clear skies and an empty stretch of sand, the only sign of life was an abandoned bonfire still aflame as though someone had prepared it and cleared the beach just for us to enjoy it. We laughed aloud, realizing this was a unique surprise. Matt pulled out a bottle of wine he bought a year before at his friend Ziad's wedding. He said he had been saving it for the perfect moment. We decided not to use our tent that night, so we put our sleeping bags next to the fire and shucked oysters and watched the sun melt into the ocean. It felt as though the universe was consipiring for us to be together.

(Left): Matt on the forklift. (Right): Picking up oysters, Oregon coast.

Matt & I at the beach, 2002

Being at ease with not knowing is crucial for the answers to come to you. ~Eckhart
Tolle

Tahoe

Inspired by my experiences on the breast cancer walk and
the tribe of people who traveled from one city to the next
doing such meaningful work, I decided it was time for a
change. Finally acknowledging the job market in San
Francisco wasn't going to rebound anytime soon, I decided
to do a 180 and become a ski instructor at Northstar in Lake
Tahoe. My friend and co-worker, Sarah, previously worked
there as an instructor, and she had a good experience, so I
thought it would be a fun adventure.

I was eager to escape the rat race in San Francisco and
trade that in for some spontaneous, carefree living. I had
spent most of my life worrying about one thing or another,
and I had been working since I was sixteen. I was hoping
some time outside in the mountains would provide some
clarity and inspiration about what I should do next. My
friends thought I was crazy for making such a hasty decision
to leave the city for a low-paying job that would do further
damage to my professional resume and possibly sabotage
future high-level corporate opportunities. I truly didn't care
what they thought, and I wasn't afraid of what I might lose.
My soul felt like it needed a big change, and I knew I couldn't
continue living in such an expensive city without a high-
paying job. I was buoyed by the memorable experiences I'd
had in South America and the breast cancer walk. I was
searching for a life of passion, but I had no idea where or if I
would find it.

One minor catch was that I wasn't that great of a skier. Actually, I had only skied a handful of times in my life and had a reputation for skiing recklessly like a bullet, without turning. My friends would give me a high five at the bottom of the mountain and say, "Wow, you're totally fearless!" The truth was I just didn't know how to turn. I couldn't find my edge, so I skied the only way I knew how – full speed down the mountain. I decided it would be a learning experience and an opportunity to develop a new skill.

I spent the following season pursuing fresh powder in my free time while making eight dollars an hour teaching people how to ski. I was so broke that winter that I couldn't afford to buy anything to heal my chapped face and hands. I was sleeping on an air mattress and rooming with girls from Australia, South Africa, and Brazil. I survived on ramen and spaghetti so that I could have the opportunity to play on the mountain every day. After the mountain closed, we would maximize our fun without rules and boundaries to keep us in check, sometimes skiing out to remote bonfires or taking snowmobiles down the mountain in the dark.

One night, the ski school team and some other co-workers from the resort met up on the mountain after dark. Grabbing lunch trays from the cafeteria, we hiked up the mountain, sat on our trays, latched our legs together and sledded down the mountain. It was so exhilarating, but I was a little nervous about what we were getting ourselves into, but we worked together as a team quickly sorting out who was in charge of steering and deciding when to detach if things went badly. We crashed a few times and once we nearly hit the lift tower, which could have ended terribly. In the end, I was really fortunate that my only wound was a long swath of skin that rubbed off my back when we crashed.

My favorite roommate, Sue, was always there for a friend in need, so she came to the rescue with some ointment. We went into the women's restroom, and we raised the back of my fleece top and pulled my pants down a little because the injury went down to my lower back and bottom. She was rubbing antibiotic ointment on my behind when we realized that the door to the women's restroom was open and a crowd of ski instructors were in the doorway, silently watching her rub my butt, trying to determine what was going on. When we all made eye contact and Sue held up the ointment, everyone erupted into laughter. I was mortified for a fleeting moment but those were good, light-hearted times.

I really bonded with the female ski instructors and was glad to find that the environment wasn't too competitive so I could learn to improve my skills without judgment. We would go out for training sessions in the powder one morning before lessons began, and the next morning they'd make us ski backwards down the mountain. We laughed so much and bonded while becoming better skiers. I was having the best time of my life, and I was really living in the moment for the first time. I found my edge, literally and figuratively. I learned how to make more efficient turns down the mountain by learning to lean onto the edges of my skis. By doing this, I was able to ski faster while maintaining better control of my turns. I felt like that was a metaphor in my own life I was learning simultaneously. If I engage in work that I'm passionate about and find my edge in real life, I'm more efficient and I have a lot more fun in the process.

I define finding my edge to be "thriving, feeling alive, and firing on all cylinders." When I was growing up, I was always worried about someone or something, and I never had the freedom or opportunity to explore life spontaneously and tap into my own passions. I was immediately hooked on that invigorating feeling. I sometimes wondered how much happier I could have been when I was younger if I had tapped into my passions at an earlier age, but there was no point in looking back.

Occasionally, one of the ski supervisors invited me to hop on the snowmobile to go put marker poles out on the mountain, or they would invite me for late-night cat-skiing, or hot-tub parties at someone's house. We made big, beautiful dinners together and woke up early to get first tracks on the powder. It felt like a dream. I became good friends with some great guys there, but I didn't allow room for anything more serious to develop because I knew deep down that my heart was taken.

Matt was traveling with his mom through Russia and Eastern Europe. He sent me pictures of frozen mailboxes and barren, icy walkways. I thought that they were probably the only people tough and crazy enough to choose to travel there in the dead of winter, and I was definitely intrigued. Then, one day near the end of the ski season, Matt emailed me that he wanted to come see me in Tahoe on his way back from his trip. I was over the moon with excitement.

The day before he arrived, a huge cold front blew in, knocking out the power all around the mountain where I lived and worked. That night, my roommates and I huddled around the fireplace, cooking grilled cheese sandwiches on a cast-iron skillet over the fire. We made the most of the situation and had fun that night, but after sleeping in the below-zero temperatures without heat, we woke up and decided that staying there wasn't sustainable.

I was so excited for Matt to meet my roommates and see our little ski chalet, but those hopes were dimming. I sent him an email to tell him I would meet him at the train station in Truckee and that we could crash on my friend's floor in town because he had power. What I didn't realize was that Matt was traveling back to the States with his mom after a late night partying with a friend in London. He was dreaming of a hot shower and a warm bed, but we slept on the dirty floor alongside eight or ten other friends that night. I don't think it was the reunion he envisioned, but he rolled with it.

The next day, I arranged for us to take some snow bikes down the mountain and play. After we tired of that, we went to the rental shop so that he could rent some snowboard boots. They didn't have any that fit his size fifteen feet, but they did have ski boots in a size fifteen. The problem was that Matt had never really skied before. This was turning out to be my lucky day. Maybe I would have a chance to inspire him and maybe even teach him a little something. I wasn't an expert skier by any means, but I could hold my own.

We rode the lift up to the top of the mountain and at one of the first junctions, there was a gnarly, double black diamond run.

He stopped in front of the run, looked at me and said, "Let's go!"

I thought he was joking at first and when I finally realized he was serious, I said, "Okay, I'll ski behind you so I can be there to pick up the yard sale that's about to happen."

Instructors sometimes did this when we felt fairly certain that the skier would lose their skis and poles on a run. It saved us having to climb back up the mountain to pick up the fallen gear.

Much to my surprise, he skied down the entire run with tight turns like someone who had done that many times. I was laughing and intrigued, but I was also a little disappointed that I wouldn't have the chance to teach him anything that day. *I was going to have to work a lot harder to find ways to inspire this guy.*

He stayed for a few days and during the day we played in the snow. When we retired to our little chalet after long days on the snow, we did our best to keep each other warm on those wicked, cold nights. On the last night, I found an envelope with a card inside it underneath my pillow. I opened the card to find a little package of forget-me-nots (the Alaska state flower), with a gift certificate for a plane ticket to Alaska.

Damn, that really took me by surprise and swept me off my feet. Matt was from Alaska and he wanted me to come visit him, meet his family and see where he grew up. I think my mouth fell open for at least a minute. I didn't know what to say. Nobody had ever given me such an awe-inspiring, thoughtful gift for no reason like that. Our time together flew by quickly, and the next morning we took the bus back to the train station. I waved and watched the train disappear down the tracks.

After Matt left, I walked down the road and met up with Sue. We decided to hitchhike to the Cal-Neva Casino & Hotel because they were advertising nineteen-dollar rooms with hot water (but no heat). We were so excited for the opportunity to take a hot shower that we jumped in with the first person to stop, feeling sure that nothing bad would happen because there were two of us.

When the man pulled up in his pickup he appeared harmless, looking like any other Tahoe guy, but he was asking too many questions for our comfort. When we finally pushed hard for him to stop the truck and let us out at the hotel, he got out of the truck with us and followed us inside. We went straight to the desk and told the woman working at reception that we were concerned about the man who followed us in, and they informed security. He turned around and left the hotel. Unlike most people who stayed at the hotel, we had no interest in gambling that night. It was cold inside the hotel, and we had been freezing for days. All we could think about were the hot showers, so when they gave us each a lit candle at the front desk, we walked up several floors to our room and stayed in, taking multiple hot showers that night. It took more than one long, hot shower to warm our bodies inside after they had been cold to the bones for several days without relief. I met such an incredible group of people through Ski School and my shared living quarters. It almost felt like, at thirty years old, I was finally living out the carefree, young adult experience I had longed for all my life.

Bluebird ski day.

(Left): Me & Sue, Lake Tahoe, CA. (Right): Me on the snow bike.

Alaska isn't about who you were when you headed this way. It's about who you become. ~Kristin Hannah

Moose Heart

As soon as the season ended, I was Alaska-bound. I couldn't wait to explore the Last Frontier and play in the snow with Matt. He was returning from a two-month trip to Thailand with some friends, and I wondered if he could possibly be looking forward to this as much as I was, after my long season of work.

I couldn't stay as long as I wanted because I had to get back to work for my next seasonal job. Between my work schedule and his off-season play schedule, we didn't have much overlapping time off to meet up, so I flew into Anchorage a few days before he got back from his trip, to go fly-fishing with some friends I met through ski school.

We busted open the ice with the little johnboat they kept behind the run-down shed they called home, and we caught rainbow trout. Thanks to the thick blanket of snow that enveloped everything, this was a quiet time of year on the beautiful Kenai River in Cooper Landing. I found it so comforting to be there after a season spent on a busy ski mountain. As we went down the river, I spotted bald eagles in the trees at every bend. Floating on the milky blue water that flowed below sheets of ice on that cold day while catching fish with good friends, I realized life has so much beauty to offer. I was so grateful for those simple pleasures.

After a couple of days of fishing, it was time to make my way to Fairbanks where Matt's family lived. His brother, Gil, kindly offered me a ride from Anchorage to Fairbanks (about seven hours of driving in the winter), so I just had to make my way to Anchorage. I decided to try my hand at hitch-hiking again, hoping I would have better luck this time.

I put my thumb out and within just a couple minutes, an old, rusty pickup truck pulled over with a gruff man behind the wheel and a young, smiley woman in the middle of the bench seat. I decided that this setup was probably as safe as I would find, so I hopped in. They asked me where I was headed and I told them Anchorage. They said that they were heading to Seward, but they could drop me off at Tern Lake, where I would have to catch another ride. *Fine by me*, I thought.

After exchanging pleasantries, the young woman asked if I wanted some moonshine.

"No thanks," I said. "I'm going to meet my friend and his family and I don't think it would be a good idea to show up with a buzz."

"Oh, come on, girl. You know you want some!" she said, erupting into a fit of giggles.

Watching them both take swigs from a bottle stowed between the driver's legs, I realized they were already drunk. *Ugh. This hitch-hiking thing was so dicey.* I wasn't up for another wild ride that day.

She offered me moonshine probably three or four more times, and she put her hand on my leg and said, "Come on, honey, loosen up a little! Everyone likes to have some fun."

I felt like such a bore, but it was early in the morning, and I had a long commute ahead of me. Plus, I couldn't help but wonder how many lips had touched that bottle.

As the minutes passed by, I grew scared and was so thankful when the truck pulled over and slowed down at the junction where our paths diverged.

"Thanks so much, you guys!" I managed. I think I actually opened the door before the truck came to a complete stop. I was so anxious to get out.

As I stood at the quiet junction at Tern Lake, I realized I was in a pretty remote area in the middle of March. It was maybe twenty degrees outside and it dawned on me that I could be there for a while.

What if nobody drives by for the rest of the day? I began to worry.

I had no cell phone service so I hoped for a safer ride, cautiously sticking my thumb out on the rare occasion that a car drove by. After about an hour of walking toward Anchorage in the cold, a minivan pulled over with five or six people from Japan and from what I could tell, they were all around twenty-five years old. They were a friendly bunch, hoping to see the Aurora Borealis. I felt sure that this was a safe ride, so I quickly jumped in and they didn't say another word to me. They blasted some techno music and danced in their seats and that was alright by me.

We pulled into Anchorage in the late afternoon. Gil offered to pick me up at a gas station there. I heard such great things about him, but I had never met him. I was nervous and hopeful that he would show up. My fears were quickly put to rest as he showed up right on time. I was so incredibly grateful to meet him there. He had a huge smile on his face and he gave me a big bear hug. He felt like family right away.

We hopped in Gil's truck and ran a few errands he needed to do before we hit the road. When we stopped by his place for a minute, I got to meet his sweet dog, Betsy, a cream-colored beagle. I think she was around eighteen years old at the time. Matt had showed me pictures of her riding in a backpack with Gil while hiking and I heard stories about her, including one about the time that they were fishing and a hook got caught in Betsy's tongue. This was a tough girl to be sure. I squatted down and gave her some cuddles, feeling so fortunate to meet this sweet pup.

We hit the road for Fairbanks. It was really dark outside, so I assumed it was late at night. When I looked at my watch, I realized it was only three thirty in the afternoon. Wow. We had so much to talk about and enjoyed looking for wildlife on the side of the road. I think I probably annoyed him, asking every five minutes whether the glowing clouds in the sky were the Northern Lights. I kept getting my hopes up, but he assured me that I would know when I saw them.

When we got to Matt's mom's apartment in Fairbanks, I felt a surreal, déjà vu feeling. Her apartment was so beautifully decorated, and I had heard so much about her from Matt that I actually felt like I had been there before. This was one inspiring woman and a kindred spirit. She had traveled to far-flung places around the world and she worked at a biology field station in college, cooking for the scientists there.

I'd heard so many stories, but one that stood out was the time that Matt, Gil, and their parents had been sleeping in a cabin, after the boys had gotten a deer on a hunting trip the previous day and hung it up in a tree in front of their cabin. Late that night, their mom awoke to some noise outside and she ran outside, wearing only her underwear and carrying a rifle in her hands, ready to shoot the suspected bear. Luckily, she didn't have to shoot anything that night, but it struck me that in a cabin full of tough Alaskan men, the woman of the house ran outside in her underwear to take care of business.

As soon as the door opened, a rush of warm air surrounded me and I could hear the faint sound of a familiar song playing. Peg gave me a big, welcoming smile and a warm hug. I knew right away that she was a kindred spirit and I would find her interesting. I was also longing to see Matt, who was standing inside behind his mom with a big smile on his face. He had such a warm, gentle way about him that made my heart feel like it was covered in honey.

We spent a few days in Fairbanks visiting with Matt's family and then drove up to Chena Hot Springs. Sitting in the hot springs, icicles formed in our hair while we looked up to find the Northern Lights on full display. Kissing him in a hidden cove of the springs that night unearthed feelings that I had never known.

We were provisioning for our trip to Wrangell-St. Elias National Park where his grandfather lived in the tiny town of

Chisana. The handful of people who lived there had established themselves there long ago and had permission from the national park to stay if they followed the rules. When visitors flew in, they needed to bring in supplies for the people living there. So, we made sure to stock up on items for the village as well as some things we needed. Flying into the harsh mountains of Wrangell-St. Elias during the winter was a new experience for me, and I didn't have the gear that was necessary to survive. I needed more layers than I was used to wearing on the mountain in Tahoe, so Matt's family generously loaned me extra clothes.

The boots they wear in the winter in that part of Alaska are called bunny boots. These extreme-cold vapor-barrier boots are used by the US military and look like big, white clown boots. They're waterproof rubber boots used only in extreme temperatures of -20 degrees F to -60 degrees F. The group told me that I had to wear them. Since I didn't own any, Matt's mom, Peggy, kindly offered me hers since she wasn't going into Chisana with us. Matt's dad, Lee, and Gil were the only ones going with Matt and me, and they all had bunny boots. I thanked Peg for letting me borrow hers, and I didn't think too much about making sure they fit properly. I was just grateful to have the protection that I needed.

We drove to Tok where the small planes flew into Chisana. Gold was discovered there about a hundred years ago, and it's registered as an abandoned ghost town. During the Gold Rush, it was the largest log cabin town in the world, but the rush didn't last long and people moved on leaving the abandoned cabins and town behind.

Since we had some downtime while we waited for the flight to leave, we headed over to Fast Eddy's, an oasis in this little roadside town with a sign that proclaimed, "No better restaurant on the Alaska Highway." We ordered breakfast from the menu and marveled over the huge plates of piping-hot food brought out to us. I asked if they knew whether you needed a CDL to drive fifteen-passenger vans in Alaska. They said no. I was looking into a seasonal job that would require me to drive a fifteen-passenger van, but I would be required to get a CDL, an endorsement that takes quite a lot of time and money.

Even though it was a Sunday morning, I asked, "Do you think there would be any way I could get an Alaska driver's license?" I didn't really have a home at the time, and the company told me I could have a license from any state. These men loved a good challenge, so they asked our server and within minutes, somebody called a woman at home who worked for the DMV. She agreed to come in and give me the test. I can't think of many other places in the world this could happen, but that's the way things worked in Tok, and I was the proud new owner of an Alaska driver's license.

I was thoroughly enjoying this opportunity to get to know Matt's dad and brother. His Dad told us a story about how he was recently talking to a woman who was afraid to use the fire escape in her building in the case of an emergency.

Lee was a firefighter, and he told her, "When those flames are licking your ass, you're gonna think it's an escalator." He was quick-witted and kept us laughing so much that we forgot how long we had been waiting.

Finally, we filled out all our paperwork for the flight and made sure the weight loads would work to bring all the gear and provisions in with us. They told us that the plane we were taking that day – an old Cessna single engine bush plane with wheel skis – was also the weekly mail plane. It had been modified for the heavy-lifting bush flying typical in this area. We loaded our gear into the plane, and the pilot let me ride shotgun with him in the front.

We took off pretty quickly, and the pilot talked to us through the headsets they provided, pointing out a herd of caribou running below, and naming countless peaks in the area.

As we were descending into Chisana, Matt pointed out a few landmarks of his own. "You see that mountain right there? That's Bullshit Ridge. Oh, and those two right there? Those are Titty Peaks. That's what Grandpa Deez calls them anyway, just so you know." "Deez" was a nickname Matt and his friends came up with because it was short for his last name, DeSpain.

We landed on the tiny snow runway in the little village of Chisana, and the handful of residents who lived there were gathered around on their snow machines, awaiting our arrival. This plane was also bringing in their mail and some of the supplies we brought in would be shared with the other residents. They were all wearing parkas with fur-lined hoods. This was the real deal. Most people who visit Alaska will never have an opportunity to experience anything like this, and I was fascinated.

When we stepped off the plane, the village residents began bantering with Grandpa Deez about what supplies we brought and what we'd forgotten. At the time, about ten people lived in Chisana, and from what I could decipher, there was a bit of a love-hate relationship among the residents. They needed each other in many ways, but the same things that brought them all there in the first place, inevitably pulled them apart. People didn't move out to a remote village like this because they're social and love to be around other people. Chisana can only be reached by bush plane or a long, arduous snow machine trip, ninety miles through mountainous terrain. The residents of this tiny village were always arguing about someone's property encroaching on someone else's or a handshake agreement that someone made about letting another person access their cabin or their gold mine. An hour later, they would all be having dinner together and laughing like nothing happened. I was enthralled, knowing I would remember this adventure for the rest of my life.

One of Matt's Grandpa's oldest friends and a resident of Chisana, Ivan, brought a snow machine out for us to use while we were there. First we gave the supplies to others who had been waiting on them, then we loaded up the remaining items onto our snow machine, and Grandpa Deez sped off to his little cabin.

Matt and I brought our supplies into the small log cabin we would call home for the week. While there was no electricity, it was clean and charming and there was a wood stove. Matt made a fire in the stove to warm the cabin, then we packed up to head over to his grandpa's cabin where we would meet up for dinner. His dad and brother were staying in a separate, much larger cabin that had electricity, but I much preferred the charm of our quaint digs.

Everyone in town used snow machines (that's what Alaskans call snowmobiles), so we rode our machines over to his grandpa's house for dinner. Approaching the cabin, it was hard for me to imagine that he had spent thirty years there. It was so small, and it looked like it was falling apart at the seams.

There were so many bumper stickers outside his front door. I tried to read them all, but most of them had faded so badly from years of harsh weather that they were no longer legible. The one I could read said "Nevermind the Dog, Beware of Owner." Matt's grandpa looked exactly like I imagined an old Alaskan gold miner would look. He had a long, gray beard and bright blue eyes that pierced right through me. He wore black-rimmed glasses, a long-sleeved shirt, and pants held up with suspenders.

I got to meet Melba, Grandpa Deez's girlfriend. I heard she was very sweet and a great cook. I was thrilled to see another woman and instantly felt relieved when I met her, as if I could go to her if I got in over my head.

When we asked if they had a refrigerator so that we could unpack a few groceries we brought, Grandpa Deez responded, "We keep most everything right under there in the cold hole." He pointed to a wooden latch in the floor.

When I opened it, I saw some old rickety stairs that led to an underground storage area. Putting on my headlamp, I proceeded to walk down the muddy stairs, then looked around and surveyed his provisions. Shelves were lined with Spam and Vienna sausages, which looked like they had been there for fifty years. I put the small supply of groceries we brought on the shelves and made my way back up to the cabin.

We gathered around the dinner table, with Rush Limbaugh turned up loudly on the radio. I thought they would turn the radio down so that we could hear each other over dinner, but I realized that the radio show was the top priority and it wouldn't be turned down for anybody.

Melba pulled some fresh bread from the oven and I was so hungry and excited for this home cooking I heard so much about. They put a piece of meat on each of our plates and everyone quietly dug in while listening to the radio. I took my first bite of meat and immediately glanced over to Matt for support. This couldn't be normal. It didn't taste right. I was a pretty adventurous eater and not one to complain, but this tasted way different from anything else I experienced before. Matt looked at me blankly. This must be normal. *I'm in trouble*, I thought. I knew I couldn't possibly finish this meat. It was really tough and had a strong gamey flavor.

About a minute later, Lee said, "Oh, Melba, this is a treat. You made my favorite meal – moose heart!"

I almost got sick right there at the dinner table. I had a bite of meat in my mouth, and it took all the strength I had to chew it up and swallow it. I was sweating and didn't feel well. I looked back over at Matt for his reaction, he just smiled blankly. He wasn't giving me any support. I managed to cut my meat into tiny pieces and had a few more bites that I smothered in jalapenos to help cover up the gamey flavor. Then I pushed the rest under a small chunk of bread I left on my plate. I didn't want to seem ungrateful, but that was the best I could do. We headed back to our cabins shortly after dinner because we had a big day ahead of us and we needed our rest.

On a clear, sunny morning we made our way to Matt's grandpa's cabin. I went inside and read the exterior thermometer. It said -22 degrees. For this time of year in Chisana, that wasn't too bad. The plan for the day was that Matt, Gil, Lee, and I would take a couple snow machines out to check on their ice-fishing holes, then build a snow shelter that Matt, Gil, and I would sleep in.

We loaded up the gear on some sleds we pulled behind the snow machines and were on our way. We were going about 30-40 mph I think, and the cold air stung my face immediately. I was wearing a neck gator, a warm hat, and big gloves, plus several layers under my coat, but it was obvious I was underdressed. I was too embarrassed to admit it and I'm not sure Matt would have heard me if I tried to say something over the roar of the engine. I had my arms around his waist, while he focused on the trail and the gear we were pulling behind us.

We made a couple stops, and I was glad to see Lee pull open the hood of one of the snow machines to warm up his hands. I could tell he had done this before and I felt safe knowing he had some tricks up his sleeve to save us if we got too cold. We all warmed our hands for a few minutes, then continued on.

We took turns driving, and I loved every second of cruising through the snow in this remote winter wonderland. We crossed lakes covered in thick sheets of ice, I winced as we drove over them. I didn't have the knowledge to trust that the ice was thick enough, and I felt sure we would plunge to our deaths. I held onto Matt tighter when we traveled over the ice, and he could tell I was nervous. They stopped their machines and insisted that I take a turn driving over the ice to build my confidence. I slowly made my way across it, but I'm not sure I felt more secure afterwards.

We checked their ice-fishing holes and picked up some gear stored in a nearby shed, then we spent a couple of hours building the snow shelter we would sleep in that night. I was baffled by the process. We shoveled loads of snow into a huge pile, then we let it firm up for a while. We then proceeded to dig out the inside of the shelter to clear a space for us to sleep that night. Suddenly it dawned on me that nobody packed a Therm-a-Rest or pads for us to put under our sleeping bags. "Matt, what are we going to use for sleeping pads tonight?"

"You don't need a sleeping pad out here. The tundra will keep you warm," Matt said, but I was deeply suspicious.

Soon after we finished building the shelter, we ran around in circles, chasing each other and trying to keep warm. The temperature reading of -22 degrees didn't account for the wind chill, and the wind was ripping. I felt naked when the wind hit my body. *I have never been this cold in my life,* I thought.

Lee decided it was time for him to take off and make his way to the warm bed in his cabin for the night, and the three of us put our gear in the snow shelter. We cooked some steaks outside and ate quickly, admiring the vast landscape before us. Gil spotted a moose and a fox in the distance, then we crawled into our sleeping bags to try to warm up while Matt stayed outside taking photographs. I thought he'd surely end up frozen into a block of ice, but when he finally made it into the shelter, the two of us zipped ourselves into one of Grandpa's double sleeping bags.

I told him I was so cold that I didn't think I could sleep, so he told me I needed to take my clothes off. I thought surely that was just a ploy or a joke, but he insisted it was true and said I could snuggle up to him and absorb some warmth that way. Against my better instincts, and growing more desperate, I took my clothes off. I couldn't believe that he was right. After a few minutes, I really did warm up a little. He also put rocks that he had warmed by the fire in the bottom of our sleeping bag and I finally managed to fall asleep for a few hours.

The next morning, we decided to explore for a while. We brought a kite with us and Matt filmed a video of Gil driving the snow machine while I was turned around backwards behind him, flying a kite. *This was the life!* We stomped around in the snow, making designs and taking pictures on a beautiful, blue bird morning.

We still had a ways to go to get back to the cabins where we were staying, which were about six miles from where we were. Since Lee had already taken one of the snow machines back, and we had packed some gear we found on the back of our sled, we realized that we wouldn't all fit on the one snow machine we had left. Someone would have to walk back, and I volunteered. The guys hesitated for a moment, then they agreed that it was fine. I appreciated that they didn't doubt my abilities. They were going to spend some more time loading up, and I was eager to soak up the majestic beauty of these mountains in solitude for a while.

I set off in the snow for my long journey and had only taken a few steps when I realized it was going to be a little more difficult than I thought. Matt's mom was six feet tall and wore a size twelve men's shoe. As if those big, white boots weren't crazy enough, they were a men's size twelve! By comparison, I wear a size seven women's shoe. There was a lot of room to spare in those crazy boots, but I wasn't going to let it stop me. I sang songs and took pictures on my way back to the cabin and tried to keep a close eye on the tracks so that I didn't get lost.

When I got back to the cabin, I realized that I urgently needed to build a fire in the wood stove or I would freeze. I found the wood supply, gathered some kindling, and started a fire. Once I got it really raging, I found a sliver of sunshine coming in from the window that fell across the bed and I took a nap. Matt woke me up when he came in, a huge grin on his face, happy that I made it and got the fire going.

That night, we rode our snow machine over to Grandpa's cabin, and I was a bit hesitant and concerned about what we would be eating. As soon as we walked in, everyone was in high spirits, laughing and gathering around. Before I could even sit down, they passed me a jar of meat and told me to try it. *Oh boy, here we go again.* I could tell this was a test, but I obliged them and took a bite of the meat, expecting something awful. I was surprised to find that it wasn't that bad.

I felt a little joy being able to tell them, "Hey, that's pretty good!" They looked at me with surprise. Their plans to rattle me weren't working. "What is it?" I asked.

Grandpa looked up at me with a smile and said, "Barbecued beaver."

Of course.

After dinner that night, Matt and I had the energy to stay up for a while, so we brought our sleeping bags out from the cabin onto the snowy runway, along with a portable CD player and speaker. We played Coldplay while we watched the most spectacular Aurora Borealis display, ribbons of red and green cascading and looping across the sky. As we laughed and reminisced about the snow shelter and moose heart, I realized that night that I was falling for this sweet Alaskan man, but our lives were on very different paths.

(Left): Flying into Wrangell St. Elias National Park on a small bush plane.

(Right): Gil & I flying a kite behind the snowmachine in Chisana.

(Left): Grandpa Deez. (Right): Matt shoveling snow to build the snow shelter.

Matt in front of the Chisana cabin.

In every walk in nature, one receives far more than he seeks. ~ *John Muir*

National Parks

Since the ski season was over, I needed to find another seasonal job. I loved the spontaneity the seasonal lifestyle provided. A friend of mine from Tahoe got me a job working for a company that led three-week camping trips through the National Parks. Thirteen passengers (mostly from Europe), a driver and myself (the Tour Guide), would travel together in a fifteen passenger van from one National Park to another, hiking by day and camping at night for three weeks. We would then drop that group off at the airport and pick up the next group. The inherent challenge with that was that I hadn't even been to some of those parks before, and I was expected to be an "expert" on them. I was very honest with my company about my lack of experience and exposure to some of these parks, but they were sure that I could "study up" and fake it until I became intimately familiar with them. I wish I had the confidence in myself that they had in me.

It was a stressful job at first, but I loved that job more than any other job I can remember. We woke up in new settings each day and I was amazed by the beauty of those remote, stunning landscapes. I also loved the long, steep hikes we took each day. We saw bears and wolves and moose in their natural habitats. The Teton mountains, Yellowstone, Yosemite, and the National Parks of Utah were among my favorite places that we visited that year. I brought my camera with me, and I lived out of the back of the van with my clothes stored in drawers below the back seat. I helped the passengers set up their tents, and we cooked meals together every day. I would then retire to sleep on the storage rack on the top of the van where I put on my headlamp and read up on the parks so I was comfortable answering questions the next day. At first I slept inside the van at night, but when I heard about a bear in Yosemite ripping the door open the back of a tour van like ours to get some provisions that had been left on the passenger seat, I switched to sleeping on top of the van. I realized that the inside of the van wasn't as safe as I thought. The roof of the van was a better vantage point for watching the stars anyway.

One day, when Petra (our driver and my new friend from Switzerland) and I were helping to load the passengers' huge suitcases and coolers full of food onto the top of the van, I fell off the roof rack. That was the first day of that particular tour, so all of those passengers who had just flown in from Europe to begin their National Parks tour had this as their first impression of their Tour Guide for the next three weeks. I was fine physically, but my self-esteem took a little beating that day.

The job also paid barely over minimum wage, so again I found myself broke and struggling to pay my graduate school debt and credit card bills. *Why was it that all the work I really enjoyed doing paid such shitty wages?* It felt so worthwhile to be doing work that I loved, but it was definitely a struggle. When I talked to my family or old friends, they thought I'd lost my way somehow with the seasonal work I was doing, but I knew in my heart that I'd found my edge climbing mountains in the wilderness. I was finally doing work that inspired me, and I didn't care what anyone else thought.

One day, a passenger hurt his toe really badly. He came to me and asked if I could rip his toenail off. We were in the Canyonlands, National Park in Utah and there wasn't a doctor's office or hospital anywhere nearby. I was a little skittish about it, but I didn't feel like I had any other choice. So, I borrowed a bottle of whiskey from one of the other passengers, and I gave him a sip of it. Then, he turned away and I ripped his big toenail off. We doctored it up a little, and wrapped it, and he felt comfortable proceeding with the trip. He was such a good sport. At 70 years of age with an injured foot, he hiked all day, every day with the rest of us without a single complaint.

We had all heard the story about a Tour Guide several years before who was taking people on a slot canyon hike through Zion National Park, and he failed to properly check the weather forecast before they departed. A big thunderstorm rolled in later that day and all eleven passengers on the tour died when the slot canyons flooded. The Guide was the only person who survived. I can't even imagine the guilt of living through that experience. There was a lot of stress and responsibility that came with the job, and we learned a lot and forged lifelong friendships over the bonds we made in the wilderness that year.

While we led those trips through the National Parks for seven months straight, we spent a great deal of time around Yellowstone National Park where we enjoyed fantastic wildlife viewing, stunning hikes to dramatic waterfalls with impossible rainbows sweeping through the canyons below. Then, we made our way to Teton National Park where we hiked Disappointment Peak and swam in the impossibly clear waters of Jenny Lake. There were a lot of sore muscles, laughter, and stories that we shared on these trips. After leaving the Tetons, we explored the National Parks of Utah, hiking through incredible slot canyons before returning the group to the airport in Salt Lake City.

We took it easy for most of the day on the last day of the tour. Our passengers wanted to do their laundry, pack their bags and contact people back home. This would also be the only day every three weeks that Petra and I could take care of our personal matters. It was the only chance to do laundry, call loved ones and pay bills. I always looked forward to this downtime so I could catch up on life and recharge my batteries.

I was exhausted and dirty, and I had been looking forward to this much-needed downtime for the past three weeks. Petra was the sweetest person and the perfect compadre for these adventures. We had to deal with difficult and demanding passengers and we did our best to keep everyone happy. She would never do anything to intentionally hurt anyone, and she was always considerate about others' feelings. So it took me by surprise to see the van pulling away from camp with my belongings inside while I was walking over in my bathing suit to collect my things. Everything I owned was in that van: my cell phone, my money, and my dirty clothes. I couldn't believe what was happening. She knew I needed my belongings during the few hours we had off before taking the group back to the airport. We had the same routine every three weeks. I took off screaming and chasing the van down the main street in Moab. My screams quickly dissolved into tears as I realized that she didn't hear me or see me and the van sped away.

That was it. My one opportunity for a few hours to make phone calls, wash my clothes, and possibly go get a coffee just went up in a cloud of dust.

The other passengers were out getting lunch, and I didn't know Petra's phone number by heart. I just sat on the curb in my dirty bathing suit in downtown Moab and cried my eyes out. It meant I would be wearing the same dirty clothes for the next three weeks, some bills might not get paid, and Mom would have to wait until the next break to hear how I was doing. I will never forget how desperate and sad I felt sitting alone without my clothes, my phone, and my money that day.

When Petra returned with the van later that afternoon, I asked "Did I do something to make you mad? Why did you leave me like that?" I asked, clearly frustrated.

She looked at me with genuine surprise and said "I thought you had already gotten your things out of the van."

It was such an honest and understandable assumption, and I instantly forgave her for leaving me behind without my things that day. We laughed so hard reminiscing over the image of me running after the van, in tears, wearing only my bathing suit. Petra lives in Switzerland and whenever we see each other or talk, we always have a long, hard laugh about what transpired that day on Main Street in Moab. I was a hot mess that day.

It wasn't lost on me that my Dad was disappointed by my choice of work. He made it abundantly clear to me that it was a big mistake, and I should climb back onto the corporate ladder and work my way back up, but I just couldn't bring myself to do it. I can't explain why, but I knew I'd found my calling out there in the quiet of the wilderness. I was fascinated by each sunrise and sunset, and each flower and rock formation unfurled a feeling of awe and wonderment deep inside of me. There was no looking back.

(Left): Me at Delicate Arch, Arches National Park, UT. (Right): Grand Teton National Park, WY.

(Left): Me in Jackson Hole, WY. (Left): Petra & I, Yellowstone National Park.

Passengers on the van, Key West, FL.

Your task is not to seek for love, but merely to seek and find all the barriers that you have built against it. ~ Rumi

In the Name of Love

Even though I was having the time of my life leading trips through the National Parks, I realized I couldn't continue living on the meager wages I was earning. The only thing that allowed me to live like that for so long was my decision to put all of my belongings into storage so I didn't have a mortgage or significant living expenses to worry about. I was definitely made for the nomadic lifestyle. I loved it, but my family continued to worry about my gypsy ways.

Since I didn't have another gig lined up yet, I visited Matt at his apartment in Phoenix. He landed a job planning the inaugural breast cancer walk in Phoenix, so he relocated there. I had some downtime, so I thought that would be a good opportunity to get to know each other better. While I was visiting him, I was applying for real jobs around the country. I needed to earn some money in the meantime, so I took a short-term gig making custom piggy banks with paint pens. I had to do something to earn cash so I could eat and pay my bills, but I couldn't escape the shame I felt each day of doing that kind of work. I didn't tell many of my family and friends about it because I was so embarrassed, and I continued to wonder how Matt saw something in me that I couldn't see in myself.

We made the most of this time together, so we'd wake up and hike Camelback Mountain or take our bikes to Papago Park and ride the trails there. The evenings were often spent on hikes through the desert, or we riding our bikes to the drive-in theatre with a tent. They let us pitch our tent up front, and we watched movies under the stars. Those were good times, but I was surprised that Matt somehow found me interesting while I was personally feeling rather lost.

One day, Matt told me to meet him by the library in Scottsdale. I still didn't have a car, so I was on my bike that day looking for jobs at the library. I rode my bike over to meet him and it was over 100 degrees outside. I made my way to the library, took off my helmet, and laid down on the outside edge of a large fountain to cool off. I dozed off for a quick nap while I was waiting for him and woke up with my head covered in fire ants. That was actually a little scary because I am allergic to ants. Matt got there just in time to witness me shaking my head violently while leaning over and scratching my head intensely. He must have thought I'd gone crazy.

He walked up and started laughing "What in the world is going on here?"

I couldn't focus on anything else, "Call a doctor."

So he called Jim, a nurse that he worked with on the breast cancer events. Jim told us to quickly get some Benadryl and see if that would do the trick and also monitor my breathing. We got some Benadryl and I began to feel better pretty quickly. *Thank goodness.* I was looking forward to our date and didn't want a headful of ants to stand in our way.

It was growing dark and Matt told me that he had plans for a picnic. We played on the love sculpture for a while goofing around and taking pictures. Then, we laid down inside the sculpture and talked. I could tell he had something he wanted to say. He waited patiently for me to stop talking about my job search and the ant fiasco. He finally got some air time, and he told me that he was "in love" with me. I was so shocked and excited to hear those words from him. I knew that he was the most special man I had ever met, so I was prepared to be patient for our relationship to grow. I was so full of love and joy in that moment. It felt like anything was possible.

I really liked the company that Matt worked for, and I was inspired to find a more meaningful job. So, I applied for a position with his company in San Diego. While I knew I was in love with Matt, Phoenix was not where I wanted to live. My bestie Tara lived in San Diego, and I had spent a lot of time there visiting her. I loved the moderate climate, beaches and laid-back vibe. I was interested in a position working with the volunteers because I had volunteered as a Crew Member for the San Francisco event, so I had a feel for what the job entailed. I felt inspired by the opportunity. A few days later, I got a call offering me a Coach position in Phoenix instead. I was a little caught off guard by the offer, mainly because I hadn't applied for a Coach position and I wasn't looking for jobs in Phoenix. So, I said that it sounded great, but I asked if it would be okay to talk to the Coach Coordinator to find out more about the position.

Later that evening, the person who offered me the position called me back and said she didn't think that I "sounded excited enough" about the job, so she rescinded the offer. *What in the world?* I was so confused and sad. I had worked in the HR field for several years, and I couldn't remember ever hearing of anything like this. I don't even remember what I said in response when she told me. I was completely dumbfounded.

I decided to go visit my Mom in Austin and figure out what my next move was going to be. When I arrived, Mom and I sat down to talk, and I just started crying right away. Mom knew me better than anyone in the world, but I don't think she had seen me cry since I was a feisty adolescent. I felt like the ground was crumbling beneath me. *What was happening to my life? Where did I go wrong? How had I gone from a successful consultant in San Francisco to this lost person I had become?* I could tell she was shocked to find me in this situation and she was having a hard time seeing me so broken. I was devastated and I desperately needed a job. I didn't even have $500 in my bank account.

Mom did what she did best that night. She made a sensational dinner of homemade shrimp ravioli, and she didn't ask too many questions. We worked together in the kitchen, and I was able to stop worry about what I was going to do about my work situation.

A few days later, Matt called me and told me there was a rodeo in Phoenix and he wanted me to come visit him so we could go together. I found this a little entertaining. This Alaskan man was inviting a Texas girl to a rodeo in Phoenix. I was intrigued, so I rented a car and drove back to Phoenix.

While I was there, I saw a job listing online for a Tour Manager for an educational exhibit at breast cancer events across the country. I couldn't believe the timing. *This is exactly what I want to do!* I would manage the tour myself and travel from one city to the next setting up a large educational Breast Cancer exhibit at 5k breast cancer runs around the country. The responsibility and pay were much better than they would have been for the Coach position. I applied, had my interviews, and they bought me a ticket to fly to Boston to begin work within a week. It was a whirlwind, but I knew that was the path I was meant to be on.

(Left) Me & Matt in the Love sculpture, Scottsdale, AZ.

I am thankful for my struggle because, without it, I wouldn't have stumbled across my strength ~Alex Elle

Mother Trucker

Jason and his boss, John, met me at the airport and took me out to dinner. They were very supportive of me, but I think they were a little nervous about my ability to do the job. I'm fairly short and it felt like they were a little concerned about a woman doing the job, but their clients who were sponsoring the exhibit really wanted a woman in that role. They explained that the next morning I would need to load up a 26' box truck then drive fourteen hours by myself to Indianapolis where the first event would take place. They were going to fly there and meet up to teach me how to set up the educational exhibit. I was so naive at the time. That night I realized that the lift gate on the truck might not be familiar to me, and I didn't want to give anyone a chance to doubt my abilities for this job. So I called Matt that night from my hotel room and asked him if he could send me a diagram of how to operate the lift gate. He loves solving those kinds of problems, so he happily hooked me up with the perfect diagram.

I arrived early to the warehouse the next day, and I think the all-male team in the warehouse were more than surprised to see me confidently operate the lift gate and use the ratchet straps to secure all of the equipment into the back of the truck. There was so much equipment that it scared me a little. I was daunted by the idea of setting up the exhibits week after week. But I finished loading everything and I set out for Indianapolis. Little did I realize there were several toll roads along the way. I incurred twenty four dollars in tolls the first day, and I was embarrassed that I was so broke and unprepared that I didn't have the cash to pay them.

I was also building my confidence behind the wheel of a huge box truck covered in pink ribbons. I used music to push my doubts away but they were still there, buried deep down. Darkness fell quickly on my first day of driving, and it was a rainy evening. I was afraid to drive too fast. There were signs that said minimum speed 50mph, so I stayed in the right lane, listening to Radiohead and trying to stay awake after a long day on the road. I was driving up a big hill, and I couldn't get the truck to go past 45mph even with the gas pedal pushed all the way to the floor. I wasn't too worried about it because I was in the slow lane. However, I noticed an 18-wheeler was driving in the fast lane next to me going about the same speed.

That's strange, I thought, but it didn't seem like a big deal. About ten minutes later, I noticed police lights in my mirror.

"You've got to be kidding me" I said audibly.

After I pulled over, I noticed another police officer had pulled over the 18-wheeler in front of me as well. I asked the police officer what was going on. He explained that I was impeding the flow of traffic.

"Seriously?" was all I could mutter. "But I was in the slow lane, driving in the rain up a hill, going as fast as I could".

He looked at me with disbelief and said "We know that you and that other truck driver know each other and were working together to block traffic behind you".

"Are you kidding? I just started a new job today, and I've never driven a truck like this before. Do you really think I'm in cahoots with the guy in that 18-wheeler? I was just doing my best to be safe, and I was surprised that he didn't pass me or go ahead of me. These aren't the best driving conditions." I explained to the officer, my mouth hanging open in disbelief.

He wasn't having it. The officers gave each of us a ticket for driving too slowly, and that pretty much summed up my first day on the job. My lip was quivering as I pulled the truck back onto the road. I kept thinking that my graduate degree really hadn't prepared me for this moment, but I refused to let my emotions get the best of me. I turned up the music and kept on trucking. After 14 hours of driving, I arrived at my hotel in Indianapolis. I was completely exhausted, but I had to meet the team before dawn the next morning to set up the exhibit. I crashed on top of the covers of my bed for a few hours.

The next day, it took us over fourteen hours to set up the exhibit. I couldn't help but think about what an exhausting national tour I had ahead of me. I would have a team of laborers in each city to assist me with set up and break down, but it was a daunting amount of work. There was a 30ft x 30ft pole tent, several educational panels that were extremely heavy with electrical wiring to assemble, and a giant, inflatable, revolving pink boxing glove on the top of the tent. The entire floor had to be covered in small rubber pieces that fit together, and we had a large plasma screen tv, a heavy desk, several tables and thousands of items to give away to breast cancer survivors.

After a long day of setting up, I woke up at about 3:30am to head out to the event, plug everything in and set things up for the day. Depending on the city, we would be expecting anywhere from 5,000-60,000 walkers to visit the exhibit for each event. I had to wear my hot pink shirt and cover up the bags below my sleep deprived eyes and share all of the energy I had left with the extraordinary people who came to these events. But I was able to dig deep into my reserves because I was passionate about the work I was doing.

I was so inspired by the breast cancer survivors I met. One of our panels was called the Wall of Hope. Survivors were able to share their stories on the wall so other people could walk through and read them. It was a very moving experience. I talked to so many women who shared their stories in tears and despair, while others were hardened by their experience and showed no emotion.

I met a survivor who lost her husband in the 9-11 attacks. She was pregnant with their daughter when she was diagnosed with Breast Cancer. I met another woman in her 70's who had beaten cancer three times already. I met a woman whose cat found her lump by scratching her several times where the lump was, forcing her to go to the doctor to get examined. The tour was a very inspirational and humbling experience.

During a short break that summer, I decided to take Mom on a trip to Mexico. Mom's 50th birthday was approaching, and I felt so much gratitude for everything she sacrificed to raise me over the years. I wanted to do something truly special for her because she worked so hard and she wasn't able to take a real vacation. I found a deal on a flight to Mexico and an all-inclusive beach hotel. I didn't ask her about it in advance. I knew that she would love it and that she needed and deserved the trip more than anything. I told her about our plans and she was thrilled. We had so much fun scheming about our trip together. We agreed to go snorkeling even though she was a bit afraid of swimming in the sea.

Flying over the aquamarine ocean near Tulum with Mom by my side, I felt a deep sense of happiness. Money and material things didn't mean much to me, but having the opportunity to treat my Mom to a trip together was priceless even though I had to use my credit card to pay for it. Over the week that we were there together, we enjoyed freshly caught seafood, shopped through the markets together, had margaritas with fresh squeezed lime juice and took boat rides to explore nearby islands.

My favorite experience from the trip was snorkeling together in Isla Mujeres. She agreed to go with me if I stayed with her. So, we swam out together, hand-in-hand, to explore the wonders of the underwater world. She was breathing so fast and so hard at first that I was afraid she might hyperventilate, but a small sea turtle swam nearby and I felt Mom's breathing slow down. I could tell she was really relaxing and enjoying the experience. We swam together for about two hours, then we swam back to the beach to dry off and have dinner. I'll never forget the joy and excitement in her eyes that day. That was a special trip for both of us.

Driving the truck.

Me on top of the big, pink truck. White Sands National Park, New Mexico.

Mom's 50th birthday. Isla Mujeres, Mexico.

The most powerful weapon on earth is the soul on fire. ~Ferdinand Foch

On the Road Again

Matt gave me some extra frequent flier miles he accrued, and I got a plane ticket to Alaska where I planned to meet up with his Mom to explore Juneau and Sitka. I also met up with our friend Christie in Skagway. Matt had to stay back in Arizona for work, but I was excited to spend some time in Southeast Alaska. The mountains meeting the ocean and cool, crisp air were a dream come true for me. During the summer, it stays light until around midnight, so we would set out on hikes and bikes rides late into the evenings. We enjoyed communal dinners with Matt's family and friends, explored glaciers, listened to live music, and went fishing on a friend's boat.

By the end of the trip, my gears were really turning. I felt sure in my heart that I wanted to live in that beautiful region, so the challenge was thinking of a way to earn a living. I thought back on my zipline adventures with Tara in Costa Rica as I walked through the woods in Alaska. I considered the possibility of building a zipline tour in Alaska, but most of the cruise ship passengers I had seen were quite a bit older. I wasn't sure if the older cruise ship clientele would be interested in doing this type of tour. There really weren't any large zipline tours that I knew of yet in the United States, so all that I had to refer to were the tours in Costa Rica. The average tourist is much younger and more adventurous there than the average cruise ship guest, but I felt as though it couldn't hurt to try.

When I flew back to Phoenix, Matt and I went out for sushi, then we played a game of pool afterwards. I decided to spring my new idea on him.

"Do you want a start a zipline tour in Alaska with me?" I asked, coyly.

Without hesitation, he said "Yes!"

I was really surprised by his response because Matt is a cautious person. He weighs things heavily and makes thoughtful decisions.

I put my hand up and said "Whoa. Wait a minute. I think you should take at least two or three weeks to think about this. Starting a business together is a huge step, and I want to make sure this is something you really want to do before we move forward."

It was funny to reverse roles with him for a moment because I'm normally the one to throw caution to the wind and he's definitely the more prudent one in our relationship. We agreed to chew on this idea for a while and check back in after a few weeks.

It was time for me to get back on the road with the breast cancer tour. Soon, I realized that the drives and exhausting labor that I was doing for each event, plus the reports, emails, and ordering was way more work than one person's job. Often, I had to drive more than the legal number of hours I was supposed to drive in one day just to make it to the next destination. I set up and worked these events around the country for about ten months, then we had two months off over Thanksgiving and Christmas before starting up again after the New Year.

The following year, I finally convinced my company that I needed an assistant, and Matt happily volunteered for the job. He was more qualified than I was with event work, but I had a year of experience managing the tour, so they kept me in my role and he got to ride shotgun with me for a year of cross-country adventures. This gave us a unique opportunity to see how well we worked together before investing in a new business in Alaska.

We met up in New Orleans around Matt's birthday to celebrate. I was driving the pink truck back to Boston to store it for the winter, and Matt met me there for a couple of days. After we got settled in our hotel, we decided to take the longboard around town, then we stopped by the House of Blues to see who was playing. We often rode double on a longboard, and it was a fun way to get around and avoid the hassles of parking. We noticed a large crowd gathering outside. I looked across the street and saw a familiar tour bus.

"No way! Willie Nelson must be playing tonight." I blurted with a little too much enthusiasm.

I had no idea if Matt was interested in seeing the concert. Matt had patiently listened to me tell him about going to see Willie play in small towns around Texas as a child. He said he would love nothing more than to go to the show with me that night, and that was all the assurance I needed. He knew that I had a soft spot for Willie. I went into a bit of a tailspin in that moment, realizing that I needed to find tickets. I told Matt I would call him when I found tickets, and I took off through the crowd asking each person if they had extra tickets.

I heard the show was sold out, but I wasn't about to give up on finding tickets. I finally stumbled on two, nice professional men who had an extra ticket. I found out from others that tickets were going for around a hundred dollars, and I was prepared to pay that price. I asked the men how much they wanted for the ticket and they asked me about my story. At the end of our little chat, they said that they wanted to give me the ticket and they wouldn't take my money because I was the biggest fan of Willie Nelson's they had ever met.

It was only at that moment that it occurred to me what I was wearing. I had work shorts and a tank top on, and I was wearing two braids in my hair with a red bandana tied around my head. I was mortified. I looked like such a poser in that crowd. I had no idea that concert was happening and if I had known, I wouldn't have been caught dead wearing braids and a bandana to a Willie Nelson concert. I looked like a crazy groupie but I let it go. I was too focused on getting tickets for the show.

Finally, I met a group of young girls who said they had an extra back stage pass, but they weren't sure if it would help us get into the show so they would only take ten dollars for it. I gave them twenty, and I called Matt to tell him we were going to the show. We made arrangements to meet on the other side of the building where it was less crowded.

Once we found each other, we noticed another tour bus nearby and Paul English walked out. He was Willie's drummer and good friend.

"Hey Paul" I said casually, feeling even more conscious of the groupie vibe I was putting out to the world.

"Hey, are you guys going to the show?" Paul asked.

"Of course" I explained how I had just scored tickets, and what happened next was so memorable.

Paul invited us onto his tour bus. Feeling self-conscious, I took off my bandana. He showed us old black and white photos of Willie and the band from the 70s, took photos with us, and signed and gave us some of those old pictures. Willie wasn't on the bus, but we had a great time with Paul, and we were excited for the show.

As we approached the stage door, we were nervous the back stage passes wouldn't work to get entrance to the show, but sure enough they let us in! We grabbed two beers and made our way to the front of the stage. We were so close that we could see the details on Willie's guitar that he called "Trigger".

That night, as we danced and sang along with the band, there were a couple times where I made eye contact with Willie, and he gave me a little smirk. I thought he was just smiling at me for no reason, but I later remembered what I was wearing and realized he may have been laughing at what a groupie I was. We had a great time that night and there was nowhere I would have rather been. If I hadn't been wearing that obnoxious bandana and those braids that day, we may not have scored tickets for the show.

(Left): Willie Nelson in concert. (Right): Me and Paul, tour bus, New Orleans, LA.

Not all who wander are lost. ~J.R.R. Tolkien

Tsunami

We had two months off before we had to report back to work on the breast cancer tour, so we decided to take a trip. I planned to meet Tara in Thailand for a couple of weeks, then Matt would fly over and we would spend another six weeks traveling through Southeast Asia together. Tara and I had a rough plan to go to Northern Thailand for a while, then head down to the beaches of Southern Thailand for the last half of the trip. We arrived there to a beautiful festival called Loi Krathong. The name means "to float a basket" and is derived from the tradition of making a krathong (decorated basket), and floating it down the river. In addition to this, people light paper lanterns and let them float up into the sky and throw firecrackers into the streets. There are also decorative floats with women dressed in silk gowns parading through the streets. It's truly a celebration like no other I've experienced. We had no idea this festival was happening, but it was our first impression of Northern Thailand and it was a spectacle to behold.

We were still a big jet-lagged, so we went to a local cafe and ordered Tom Yum Goong. This is a simple broth soup with shrimp that I had enjoyed many times before. It's normally pretty spicy and Tara and I both have a pretty high tolerance for spice, so we naively told the waitress that we would like it at a level 4 spice out of 5. Back home, that would have been just right. But the soup they brought us literally brought tears to our eyes. We blew our our noses and had tears running down our faces for the entire meal.

We decided to visit an elephant sanctuary the next day. So many people visit Thailand and ride elephants that are treated badly and kept in captivity. We didn't want to take part in that experience, so we visited a sanctuary where we spent the day learning about the rescued elephants and enjoyed watching them walk around freely with their babies. We got to help bathe the baby elephants in the river. That was a joyful experience.

We also signed up for a Thai cooking class. This was such a sensational highlight of the trip for me. The classes took place on a covered veranda attached to a local family home. We were able to enjoy a glass of wine while learning to cook some incredible Thai dishes, then we got to savor the food together with our new friends and got a copy of the cookbook to take home. I was hooked on this lifestyle and I could see myself staying there indefinitely. We made our way to the beaches of Southern Thailand where we enjoyed long-tail boat rides, snorkeling and rock climbing at Railay and Krabi beaches. We then continued on to Koh Phi Phi where we enjoyed the crystal clear beaches and a vibrant nightlife scene.

After a couple days in Koh Phi Phi, Matt arrived and met us there for one night together before Tara took a ferry and made her way back to Bangkok. The night that Matt arrived, I took my first dose of doxycycline for malaria prevention because we were planning to visit some remote areas. The next morning I woke up with a golf ball sized welt on my forehead. Tara and Matt looked at me with big eyes and asked me what happened. I had no idea what they were talking about, so I went into the bathroom to take a look.

"Damn. That's crazy. Do you think it's a spider bite?" I asked.

We all agreed that is probably what it was, but we had no idea whether it was serious or not, so we decided I would walk over to the local clinic to have it checked out. The clinic was outside and stray cats were walking all over the tables and beds. When I finally got to speak to a doctor, they thought my boyfriend hit me.

"Seriously?" was all I could say. Matt was the most gentle soul who saved poisonous insects instead of killing them, and I was offended that they would suggest otherwise.

Speaking of insects, I asked about local spiders, but they assured me that no spider there would make a welt like that. So, we just shrugged it off.

We saw Tara off to the ferry and we made our way to the next island, Koh Tao where we enjoyed fire dancing and fresh smoothies. We stayed in a total dump where the toilet was just a hole in the floor. The room had no air conditioning. There were mosquitos flying around the room and the only protection was blasting the fan so hard that it prevented them from landing on our bodies. There was nothing romantic about that room, so I asked Matt when he had been to Thailand with an old high school friend of his whether they ever stayed in a room that was worse.

He said "Oh no, we never stayed in anything this bad. Ted always preferred to stay in rooms with air conditioning and television."

I was shocked to hear that he stayed in places that were so much nicer with his friend yet he assumed I would enjoy roughing it. I knew deep down it was a vote of confidence in my tolerance for those situations and our shared love for adventure and great stories, but I insisted after that experience that we "splurge" on a place for $10 instead of $5 once every week or two, and I'm glad we did. We ate dinner on the side of a tall cliff that hung over the ocean and watched the sunset while ordering whole local fish prepared any way we liked. I decided that our rooms didn't matter that much if we could have experiences like that.

We made our way out to the Surin Islands. The islands were hard to reach at that time. We had to search for a while to find a boat that would take us there. It was a small speed boat that took several hours to bring us to our landing spot. The accommodations were tents, and we were surrounded entirely by Thai people. There were no foreigners in sight. We walked over to the outdoor cafeteria, and we noticed the whole menu was in Thai and there was nobody available to translate for us. We chose items at random, paid less than two dollars for our food and it was insanely delicious. We made plans to go out on a long tail boat ride the next day for a snorkeling adventure. The tours cost only a couple of dollars because they were provided by the park service. We went out for the best snorkeling trips of our lives over the course of the next couple days. One day while we were out snorkeling far away from shore, the boat driver dropped us all off in the water and they somehow left us behind when they picked everyone up.

"How could they forget the only white foreigners on the boat?" we debated.

After the boat left and the sun was setting on the horizon, the boat finally came back for us and I breathed a sigh of relief. We were in great spirits on the boat ride back that night, realizing what the alternative ending could have been for us. When we got back to our tent, I realized that I had some blisters on my chest. They looked like jellyfish stings. We couldn't figure out what else could have possibly caused the blisters, so I walked over to the medical tent and talked to a doctor. I asked if the blisters could have been from jellyfish, but they said they didn't have stinging jellyfish in the area. We were puzzled but nobody had any explanations for us, so we just let it roll off our shoulders.

We went back to the mainland area of Thailand the next day where we had a nice dinner before trying one of the banana crepes that the street vendors made. There wasn't much that tasted better than that. To top off the evening, we signed up for massages. We got massages every few days while we were there because they were normally just five dollars or less. Two women picked us up on motorcycles to bring us to their massage area in the back of a bridal dress shop. It felt so satisfying to live in the moment and really absorb those unique and joyful moments. I was loving every second.

After our massages, we were walking through town, and we saw a little travel agency shop. We walked in to inquire about prices on flights or bus rides to Laos where we decided to spend Christmas. We left early the next morning to explore Laos and Vietnam even though our return flights home left from Bangkok. We agreed to return to Thailand at the end of our trip to spend some more time in the area before we left the country.

We took a bus to Laos the next day and spent Christmas in Luang Prabang. The day after Christmas, we saw a small television screen with BBC News saying there was a tsunami that hit earlier that morning and "four-hundred fisherman were missing". That was the extent of what we saw about the tsunami at that point. Nearly two-hundred and thirty thousand people died from the tsunami, making it one of the deadliest human tragedies in modern history. We were not staying in rooms with televisions and since there was a language barrier, we didn't understand much of the conversations around us. It wasn't until the next day that we realized the magnitude of the situation. We immediately realized how worried our families must have been, so we made tireless efforts to reach them. We didn't have cell phones with us, so we had to use phone booths. Some of the phone lines didn't work, or they were busy, so it took a while to get through to our parents. They were overwhelmed with relief when we finally got through. My Mom had already called the US Embassy. We felt badly that so many hours had passed before we found out the extent of what happened. We spent the better part of that day emailing all of our extended family and friends to let them know we were okay. Everyone thought we were still in Koh Phi Phi because we had sent out an email update from there just a few days beforehand and at that point, we didn't have any plans to leave. We'll always be grateful for the intuition that led us to leave when we did. We could have easily spent the whole trip in that tropical paradise.

We felt sick about everything we were seeing in the news. We got to know the local boat operators and met their families, and we befriended many people in the villages, and it was mind-boggling to process that those villages had been entirely swept out to sea. We wanted to go back and help in any way possible. We spent a solid day or two reaching out to organizations in Thailand and doing research online. Unfortunately, at that early stage, they were only allowing people with ten years of disaster recovery experience to help. They were only at the point of recovering and identifying bodies, and they needed doctors and experienced relief workers. We felt helpless and spent some time thinking about the gravity of what had happened. It was difficult to process. We decided to head to the mountains and rivers of Laos to unwind a little. We ended up spending a couple of weeks there before making our way to Vietnam.

We flew into Hanoi where I was intoxicated by the smells and energy that flooded the streets. Crossing the streets there was an adventure of its own. You basically had to just go for it and walk at the same pace the whole time. If you got scared and slowed down or stopped, you would most likely get hit by a motorcycle. I was excited to check out some of the local Vietnamese food as it had always been one of my favorite cuisines. We made our way down some alleys and found a great little restaurant that served pho. We each ordered a bowl and sat down to enjoy them together. I tried to eat a bite but my esophagus felt like it was swollen shut, I just couldn't swallow. I had to leave a bowl of piping hot goodness sitting in front of me. What a tragic moment that was for me. I had been waiting to try local Vietnamese food for the whole trip, but now I didn't feel well enough to eat it! We sat next to a doctor from the US, and he asked if we were taking any medications. I explained that we were taking doxycycline and he immediately said that I might be having an allergic reaction to it.

We walked over to an internet cafe where Matt ordered a banana smoothie. We hopped online to do some research, and sure enough we saw the information about allergic reactions to doxycycline. The first level reactions were swelling of the head, hands and feet. The next level reactions involved blisters that often appeared on the chest. After that, people sometimes experienced swelling of the esophagus, anaphylactic reactions, followed by a "BLACK, HAIRY TONGUE!"

Matt literally dropped his smoothie when he read that but what caught my eye even more was the line below it that read "death". We immediately stepped outside onto the busy streets of Hanoi and climbed into a tuk-tuk. It should have cost us only two dollars for a ride to the hospital, but Matt misunderstood the price to be twenty dollars through a stressed miscalculation, so he gave the driver twenty dollars in Vietnamese dong, and we hopped out.

Just as we got out of the tuk-tuk, a serious motorcycle accident happened right in front of us. We helped carry the injured guy into the hospital, then we tried to get help with my problem. They were too overwhelmed so they sent us to another hospital. At the Americanized hospital we were referred to, they tried to tell me that they thought I must have swallowed a fish bone. They were convinced that must be what was wrong with me and why I couldn't eat anything. They tried to force me to do a $350 lung and heart X-Ray. I had been climbing, rappelling, hiking, and swimming vigorously each day. I was sure that my heart and lungs were fine, so I refused the X-Rays and they made me sign a waiver saying that I wouldn't sue them if I died as a result of refusing the X-Rays. Finally, I was able to talk to a doctor about the medication I had been taking and they admitted that there were people who had rare, but very serious (even deadly), reactions to doxycycline. So, we agreed that I would stop taking the medication right away, and they finally gave me something to help provide some relief to my esophagus. By the end of the next day, I felt much better and I was able to eat again. I savored the flavors of a delicious Banh Xeo. Thank goodness we figured out that mystery, and I managed to avert the black, hairy tongue!

We made our way south to Hoi An where we enjoyed culinary delights like white rose dumplings and we had custom clothes made for us. This was such a novelty to me because I'm not much of a shopper. One morning, as I was still sleeping, Matt came back to our room and woke me up to tell me that I needed to go shopping. Honestly, I thought I was dreaming at first because Matt isn't much of a shopper either so those are the last words I expected to hear from him.

"What are you talking about?" I looked at him suspiciously.

"There are these shops where you pick out any design and the material that you want, and they make custom clothes for you in one day." I could see the excitement in his face and that intrigued me.

I still wasn't feeling one hundred percent better since my reaction to the doxycycline, but I mustered the energy to get up because it was rare to see Matt this excited about something. It piqued my interest even more because I had never seen him get excited about clothes.

We walked to the town-center and made our way into a shop that had several large tables in the middle. The walls were lined with shelves from floor to ceiling that were covered in material, ranging wildly in color and texture. There were giant piles of magazines stacked haphazardly on the tables. The idea was that customers would choose a photo of an outfit, pick the material they liked, then they took the client's measurements. The very next day, the custom-tailored clothes would be ready. It was truly awe-inspiring. I really struggled to pick out something because I wasn't in the headspace and I didn't care about clothes very much, but Matt was knee deep in plans to have a suit made. What always amazes me about him is that he is so frugal about things like hotel rooms, food and buying older, used cars. But when he sees a unique opportunity, he is always willing to invest in it. I love that about him. We were staying in some really rough places, but he was having a suit made with custom shirts and ties. I was trying to think about what I wanted to have made and I finally decided on a Vietnamese silk dress and a red and gold silk robe. We picked up our clothes the next morning and we were thrilled with how they turned out!

After that, we took a long bus ride to Mui Ne where we spent the day sledding the giant sand dunes, then we watched the locals fish with their big nets, marveling over the round baskets that women rode around in on the water. We couldn't understand how they could navigate those little round baskets, but they made for interesting photographs.

Our next stop was Da Nang where we stayed in a little cabin in the mountains. The reason we made the long journey to Da Nang was for the fantastic canyoning and rappelling. We spent a couple of days exploring and rappelling down the area's mountains and waterfalls and enjoying the local cuisine.

We made our way through Ho Chi Minh and finally returned to Thailand. Tourists were still forbidden to go near the beach areas on the west coast affected by the tsunami, so we spent a few days in Ko Chang on the east coast. This was a quiet fishing village at the time and they were not accustomed to large droves of tourists rolling in. However, since the tsunami, thousands of tourists were diverted from the overcrowded beaches of places like Phuket to these remote, quieter islands. The local community was doing their best to manage. There were signs outside the tiny restaurants that read "Expect wait times of up to 2 hours. Doing our best." I was shocked to see American tourists complaining about the wait times for their food. I ran back to our room to get some books that I had recently finished. I gave them to the restaurant so they could offer them to their guests who were waiting. I explained how happy we were to be there and told them we were totally content to wait as long as it took to make our food. We tipped them generously and headed out to walk back to our room.

I saw a street vendor selling cloth hammocks, I had been thinking about getting one for a while. I noticed the price was a little higher than we saw on the west coast of Thailand but I decided to buy it anyway. While the Thai woman was getting my change, another American woman walked up with her husband, and she was aggressively harassing the woman about her prices. Mind you, the price I paid for the cotton hammock was about $8 USD, so these prices were still killer by American standards. The Thai woman who worked the booth was pregnant and she made the items herself. She was very sweet and patient. The American woman told her how much cheaper the hammocks were in Bangkok, then aggressively complained about the prices. The Thai lady quietly listened and didn't engage in the conversation. It was easy to tell that she wasn't able or willing to go down on her prices, or she most definitely would have offered to negotiate. I'd learned from talking to her that her extended family was still not accounted for since the tsunami, and she had an understandably sullen demeanor.

I stepped into the conversation and said to the American woman "You've made your point, and it appears that these are the prices for her merchandise. If you see something you want to buy, great. Otherwise, please leave this sweet woman alone. She would tell you if she could go down on her prices."

The Thai woman hugged me and there were tears of gratitude in her eyes. I was horrified watching tourists invade these quiet little islands demanding five-star food, accommodation and service from people who were still suffering the fallout from a devastating tragedy. They were simply absorbing the overflow from other areas and most of the communities had been severely impacted by the tsunami. They lost family and friends and there was a shortage of supplies and food. It felt as if the tourists there hadn't heard about the enormous devastation that impacted the country just a few weeks beforehand. It's shocking how some people really have a lack of compassion and empathy.

Our last night was spent in a tiny old bungalow over the ocean. You could see the jade colored water through the wooden planks on the floor. This was the nicest $2 room we stayed in on the trip, although there was still no air conditioning or television. It was really basic but it was perfect for us. We enjoyed a nice seafood dinner, then walked out to the end of the nearby dock and sat down to watch the sunset. Tears were streaming down my face and Matt asked me if something was wrong.

I looked up at him, barely able to speak "Not at all. I just love it here so much, I don't want to leave."

Rickshaw ride, Vietnam.

(Left): Me on a junk boat in Ha Long Bay, Vietnam (Right): Matt in Ha Long Bay

Me sand-sledding, Vietnam.

You were never Red Ridng Hood. You were always the Wolf. ~Abby
Wombach, WOLFPACK

The Last Frontier

We flew back to the States the next day and jumped right into work with our first breast cancer event of the season. I'll never forget our first night in bed in the hotel.

Matt said "I feel like we stole a truck and a credit card". He was clearly so happy to be traveling around the country, seeing new places, doing educational work and getting paid pretty well to do it. I was so happy to have him by my side.

We put all of our belongings into storage and Matt sold his car. I hadn't owned a car for six years, so I had a pretty light load. Since neither of us owned a home or car at the time, we were able to really minimize our expenses. We learned quickly not to blow the per diem we received for meals. We stuck with a tight budget and we tried to find hotels that had great reward programs and offered a free breakfast. We normally shopped for simple lunches from grocery stores and shared a meal from a restaurant for dinner.

After a couple months, it became evident how quickly we were able to save a significant amount of money. Since we were working and traveling together, we were able to spend all our free time talking about the idea of starting a zipline tour in Alaska. Matt never wavered with his interest in starting this business together, so we were full steam ahead by this point. We spent hours discussing the business while we were driving cross country from one event to the next.

We decided that Juneau made the most sense for our tour, mostly because Matt had family there and it was the largest city in Southeast Alaska, so we could get supplies more easily too. We had a break from the tour for about six weeks that summer, so we decided to spend that time in Juneau looking for land.

"Zipline" is a common name people use to describe a tour where people wear a harness and lanyard and clip into a pulley on a cable and slide from one side to another. A canopy tour is a type of zipline tour built in the trees. People take off from, and land on, platforms built into the trees. The tour we were planning to build was technically a canopy tour, but for the sake of simplicity, I will refer to the tour as a zipline tour because that is the common name and more inclusive term that people are more familiar with in the United States.

Since we had to save every penny we'd earned to build our zipline tour, we couldn't afford to stay in hotels during our summer off of work. So, we decided to camp in Juneau for the entire break. People think living off the land in Alaska sounds adventurous and exciting. In reality, it's cold, wet and the sun often shines through the tent at night so it's difficult to sleep. If you haven't spent time in Southeast Alaska, you really can't fully appreciate the inherent weather challenges. It rains a lot. There are summers when the temperature doesn't get above the 60's and it's pretty much raining most of the time. Camping in those conditions for a long period of time isn't for the faint of heart. Mark Twain once said "The coldest winter I ever spent was a summer in San Francisco." When I lived in San Francisco I thought that made sense but that was before I spent a summer camping in Alaska.

We bought a tent at the REI Garage Sale Event in Seattle before we got to Alaska. Matt really wanted a tent that he could stand up in, and he's six feet, five inches tall, so that didn't leave us with very many options. Thankfully, we found the perfect tent. It was a slightly damaged tent made by Sierra Designs that was almost seven feet tall inside. We bought her, called her the Taj Mahal and made plans to have her fixed up in time for our big adventure.

We also bought a portable grill and decided that we would catch all of our protein that summer to save on our expenses. We bought our fishing gear once we arrived in Juneau as well as some Xtra Tuf rain boots. Locals call Xtra Tufs "Alaskan Tennis Shoes", and I can understand why because there is something comfortable and utilitarian about them. My Xtra Tufs were my third pair of shoes. I owned a pair of hiking boots and a pair of flip flops, and I honestly felt like there weren't any other shoes I could possibly need.

Matt and his Dad shared the sixteen-hundred dollar expense for an old Mazda pick-up truck a few years back and the truck stayed with his Dad in Alaska. His Dad agreed that it was Matt's turn to take it. We flew to Fairbanks and picked up the truck. We dubbed her "the Little Engine" because she was such a reliable old girl. While we were there, we were looking at camper shells for the back of the truck so we could keep our belongings dry. Matt's Dad noticed what we were doing and he very generously offered to buy a camper shell for us. The only one that fit the old black truck was an old, pink camper shell that looked like the color of Pepto Bismol and was slightly longer than the bed of the truck. I can't tell you how grateful we were for that camper shell. It was a thoughtful gift that would come in very handy. A few days later, we made our way to Juneau.

We arrived in Juneau by ferry and met some interesting people on the ride over. We were thrilled to make a connection with some great local people. When we told them we were going to camp the whole time, they sized us up a bit and said "Good luck".

We drove to the Mendenhall Campground, situated alongside the banks of Mendenhall Lake with a beautiful view of the Mendenhall Glacier. *Not a bad start to the summer*, I thought. We were on an adrenaline high from the excitement of it all. We found our spot and got situated. After we pitched our tent, we read over the campground rules.

"Camping not allowed for more than fourteen days". *What?!* We had clearly made a rookie mistake by not researching this detail ahead of time. We had six weeks of camping ahead of us. We did some more research and found out there was another campsite nearby and we were allowed to go back and forth between them, but we could only stay at one for fourteen days at a time. *Oh boy.* That made things a lot more complicated, moving our home back and forth, but we decided it was just a small bump in the road. We walked to the edge of the lake and had some crackers and cheese, then got some much needed sleep.

The next morning, we headed to Fred Meyer for provisions. We needed a lot of things, and first on the list was black paint and a paint roller. We had to do something about the Pepto Bismol-colored camper shell. We picked up some basic groceries and water, as well as fishing licenses and a cooler. We headed back to the campground on that beautiful, sunny day and played music while we hand-rolled black paint on the camper shell, giddy over the possibilities ahead.

Occasionally on the day we would have to move from one campground to another to avoid overstaying our two-week limit, it rained so hard that we didn't have the energy to set up camp in the rain. When that happened, we pulled the truck over on a quiet street and slept in the front seats with hope that the rain would subside soon and we could set up camp again without our gear getting soaked in the process. We hung our rain jackets over the windows in hopes that it would be harder for people to see us inside.

We made an appointment with the Small Business Development Center and met with a lovely woman named Jackie. I wanted to seek her help with writing a business plan for our zipline tour, and she was very kind and helpful. Her first suggestion regarding land for the tour was at the local ski area. It seemed to make sense to use an area that was already designated for recreational use. That way, we wouldn't be disturbing people in residential areas. I worked with her for a couple weeks to develop a summary of our plans, then we made an appointment to meet with the Ski Manager. Our biggest concern was that he would share our idea with someone else who would take the idea and do it on their own. At the time, there weren't any zipline tours in the US that we were aware of although we later found out there was one in Hawaii and one that was just built in another city in Alaska.

We presented our idea to the Ski Manager, and we gave him a five-page summary of our plans. After we were finished with our presentation, and he had asked us some questions, he paused for what felt like an hour.

Then he said "Let's make this happen."

I looked at Matt as if to say *Did you just hear what I heard? Did he really just say that?* Then, the manager explained that it wouldn't be easy. We would have to get nearly ten permits, plus we would have to present our idea to the city planning committee, then they would vote on whether or not they found this Conditional Use acceptable. If approved, we would have to borrow some money because we didn't have quite enough saved to cover all the expenses, and we had to build the damn thing. But finding a location was a huge part of the equation, so we were shocked by how smoothly that initial meeting went.

We went back to our campsite and made plans to celebrate with some Glacier-Ritas (margaritas made with glacier ice). First, we needed a piece of ice, so we walked down to the edge of the lake with our axe. We were going to wait for a piece of ice to float to the edge, then use the axe to chop the ice into a reasonable size to put into our cooler. We had a blender and an inverter that we plugged into the cigarette lighter in the truck. After about thirty minutes, we realized that the ice wasn't going to just float over to the edge of the lake for us to harvest. We needed to wade out into the water to collect it. I was still wearing my Xtra Tufs, and somehow Matt decided I should be the one to go in the ice-cold lake to get the ice.

"Fine. I'll do it" I said without putting up a fight.

I walked carefully in until the water got close to the tops of my boots.

"I can't reach it" I said in frustration.

"Just go a little farther" he said, obviously laughing.

I didn't care about getting wet or cold. I was determined to get that ice if it was the last thing I did. I took another step and my boots filled with water, then I proceeded to chop some ice for our cooler. It's astonishing how much sacrifice and energy I put into something that I could have bought at the store for $2.00.

After we finished up the breast cancer tour, we decided to move all our things to Juneau. There's nothing like diving into the unknown. We had no idea if our idea would be approved by the city, or whether we could get all the necessary permits and raise enough money, but we were going to die trying. One of the biggest challenges was figuring out how to get to Juneau with all of our belongings. We decided to buy a fifteen passenger van from the company I worked for when I led the camping treks. The van even came with the large roof rack still attached that would allow us to haul more of our stuff. We later dubbed her "Ol' Yeller", but we realized it wouldn't quite fit all of our gear.

Matt's Dad asked him if he would be willing to pick up a pontoon boat for him and bring it up to Alaska because he had plans to build a fish wheel on top of a pontoon boat so he could catch salmon on the Copper River, making use of his subsistence fishing permit. Fish wheels are devices operated in rivers to catch fish that look and work like a watermill. They are outfitted with wire baskets to scoop fish from the river and drop into a holding tank. Sometimes, subsistence fishing from a fish wheel could yield hundreds of fish per day. We agreed to bring a pontoon boat to Alaska for Matt's Dad and decided we could put a few of our things into the pontoon boat to transport across the country to our new home in Alaska at the same time.

We drove the van to Texas to see my family where we also picked up the pontoon boat for Matt's Dad. Once we had that set-up ready, we made our way to Phoenix to get Matt's belongings out of storage. Then, we drove to San Francisco to get my things out of a tiny pod. When we got to my storage unit, our space in the van was already limited.

Matt said, very matter-of-factly, "You're gonna have to throw some of your shit away."

That really wasn't very much like him to say something that sounded so callous, so I decided to crawl into my sleeping bag on the deck of the pontoon boat and take a nap in protest.

When I woke up, I realized that I was going to have to give up some of my things. The first thing Matt nominated was a steel and concrete table that my ex-boyfriend made for me. It was a really nice table, but I reluctantly agreed. The next item on the chopping block was my favorite reading chair. That wasn't an easy process; it was almost midnight and we had been driving all day. Finally, we fit the small amount of things we deemed to be a priority into the van and boat and made our way towards Seattle. We made a stop to get gas before too long. Matt wanted to climb up on the rack to rearrange some of our things and secure them a little better for travel. When I glanced up to check on him, I saw that he had fallen off the top of the van and I made a wild noise that Matt described as the sound a mother tiger would make if she watched her baby die. He popped up and said he was just fine. So, we hit the road again.

It was early December, and we were nearing the Alcan Highway where there would likely be lots of snow. We were motivated to get to our destination as soon as possible because we had a set day and time to meet Matt's parents in Whitehorse to give them the pontoon boat and catch the weekly ferry to Juneau. When we arrived at the Canadian border, the Border Patrol guard gave us a suspicious look. Of course he did; we looked like the Beverly Hillbillies. We were directed to pull over and go inside the building. We spent the next several hours talking to the Border Patrol

Officers while they searched our belongings. Finally, they gave us their approval to cross the border.

Not long after we made our way into Canada, it began snowing. It was actually dumping snow with blizzard conditions. Since we had a schedule to keep, we couldn't afford to wait it out, so we drove late into the night in the snow. We couldn't drive very fast, but we decided to do the best we could.

About two hours into the drive the next day, we noticed something wasn't right, so we pulled over. We had a flat tire on the trailer. The trouble was that we were in the middle of nowhere. We had to detach the trailer and drive thirty minutes to the next small town where we found someone to open the tire shop and sell us a tire. Then, we had to make our way back to the trailer to change the tire and hook the trailer back up to the van again. The following morning, we did our daily inspection of the boat and noticed the motor on the back of the pontoon boat was creating a lot of stress on the boat.

We needed to move the three-hundred fifty-pound motor off the back of the boat. It was too heavy, and it was causing the pontoons to collapse. We called some shops in the next town to see if someone had a fork-lift we could use to move the motor. Finally, we found a local guy who agreed to rent us his personal forklift. Matt had to disconnect the motor in the snow in the dark, then lift the motor off the back of the boat with a forklift and put it into the boat. This took us a few hours in negative forty-degree weather, then we continued driving late into the night.

Our hope was to meet Matt's parents in White Horse a day or two before our scheduled ferry departure from Haines. However, it was becoming abundantly clear that we would be fortunate just to make it to White Horse in one piece, unload our things from the boat into a storage unit so we could come back for them at a later time, then grab some food and say our goodbyes so we could catch the ferry from Haines to Juneau. The winter ferries didn't operate as often, so if we missed the ferry it meant we would have to pay for lodging for about a week before the next one departed.

When we arrived in Whitehorse to meet Matt's family, Matt and his Dad immediately made a makeshift ramp out of plywood, and we all took turns carrying things down from the boat into the storage unit. Then we had some hot tea and lunch, gave his parents a big hug and continued driving. We were so relieved that we made it to Haines barely in time to catch the ferry.

(Left): Goofing around w/ Matt in front of the pink truck. (Right): Getting ice.

Me & Matt with our business license at the campground.

(Left): Our pickup truck w/pink camper shell. (Right): Sleeping in the front of the truck.

Me & Matt, Juneau, AK (2005).

Me on top of the van, adjusting gear with the pontoon boat in tow.

Camping, Denali National Park, AK.

Where we come from is who we are, but we choose every day who we become. ~JD
Vance (Hillbilly Elegy)

Leap of Faith

We arrived in Juneau on a cold evening in December.
Matt's Uncle Al and Aunt Pam let us stay at their house for a
couple of days before we moved into a home where we
would be house-sitting for a while. We literally walked in, set
our bags down and fell asleep on the floor next to the
heater. We were so relieved to have made it to our
destination safely and we needed to recharge our batteries.

We were so grateful for the opportunity to house-sit in
their lovely home overlooking the Gastineau Channel and
downtown Juneau. We needed to put every dollar we had
saved into the new zipline tour we were going to build and
we had to borrow some money as well to pull it off, so we
didn't really have money for rent at that point.

We hit the ground running. We spent our days writing
extensive business plans, building a website, writing potential
investors, filling out permit applications, researching builders,
learning about industry standards, joining local community
organizations and so much more. We went to the public
library and wrote down all areas of the business that needed
attention. We decided on sixteen categories. We each took
eight categories and agreed not to step on each other's toes
because there was too much work to get done to be
overlapping on anything.

Soon, our city meeting was scheduled where members of
the community would come in to speak their minds about
our project. If there was a lot of protest, that would have
meant the end of the road for our plans. The meeting was

set for Valentine's Day at 7:00pm. That was definitely a unique way to celebrate our love.

Our Aunt Judi came to the meeting to share her support and just after she spoke, she had some significant chest pains and had to go to the hospital. Thank goodness, it wasn't too serious, but we were really concerned about her when she fell ill during the meeting.

After an exhausting evening of answering questions and listening to concerns and comments, we were finished. They issued us a Conditional Use Permit to use the land at the local Ski Area to build our zipline tour. It was a huge accomplishment, and I wanted to feel excited, but I couldn't escape the heavy burden of work ahead of us.

We had already flown our prospective builder out to Juneau to give us an estimate for the project. So, the next step was to hire an Arborist to evaluate our trees to determine if they would be sufficient and capable of holding the steel cables and platforms. The Arborist was a smart, outdoorsy guy who seemed comfortable with our plans. That was a great start because most people at the time hadn't heard of a zipline, and they looked at us like we were crazy when we shared our concept. After he climbed the first couple of trees, he lost his balance and fell. It wasn't too dangerous because he was clipped into a point on the tree and he had a shock absorber, so he was dangling a couple of stories up in a Sitka Spruce tree while he caught his breath. I was worried about him.

"Area you okay?" I asked.

He began to make his way down. "That's it for me you guys. I'm spent"

He glanced over at Matt and I when he got back to the ground, and we could tell that we needed a back-up plan.

"What if I were to climb the trees with your tool and collect the core samples for you to evaluate?" I sheepishly offered.

We didn't have much in the way of time or money to spare, so that just seemed like the easiest way to allow him to complete the analysis.

"That's fine with me" he offered with resignation.

So, I pulled on my harness, clipped into the climbing gear and made my way up the next tree about sixty feet above the ground. I collected the sample, feeling rather proud of myself. Matt gave me a supportive nod from below and I reached back to put the sample back in my tool belt. Unfortunately, I missed the pocket because I couldn't see behind my back and the tool slipped out of my hands and fell into the snow below the tree. I rappelled down and we spent the next several hours looking for the tool. Thankfully, Matt finally found the tiny straw-shaped tool just a moment before we vowed to give up hope. It was about twenty degrees outside and it was growing dark. We decided to return the next day to collect the rest of the samples. The trees were deemed healthy and the builders got their plane tickets to come out and help us build our tour.

We were up working all hours of the day and night, but there was so much hope and possibility on the horizon. The first cruise ship was due to arrive in Juneau around the end of April and we only had six weeks to build the tour, hire our guides, buy all of our gear, and train everyone before then. We couldn't afford to fall behind schedule.

The night before our builders arrived, Matt and I went out to dinner at our favorite local spot. We were overflowing with love and excitement about building a business of our own that we were so passionate about. Then, we went back to the house and laid down in bed. Matt rolled over and pulled out a ring that he had hand-carved from wood from a tree near the tour we had built. I looked up at him to make sure this meant what I thought it did. I was in such a state of shock that it took a couple minutes for me to answer him when he asked me to marry him. There was no doubt in my mind that the answer was yes. He was the love of my life, the most handsome man I'd ever seen, the kindest soul I'd ever known, and my very best friend. There was just so much happening, and I wanted to fully soak the moment in. Not only were we about to start a zipline business together, we were going to get married! I felt like the luckiest girl in the whole entire world, and my heart felt like it was going to fly out of my chest.

That night as I was falling asleep, my thoughts kept drifting back to a younger version of myself who lacked self-esteem and didn't feel worthy of love. It was almost as though I was trying to channel thoughts back to that little girl to say "It will all be okay. You will find your way, and you are worthy of love."

The crew arrived the next morning to almost three feet of fresh snow on the ground. I was doing my best to get my head out of the clouds from the news of our engagement, but it was hard. My family and friends were all calling to give their congratulations, but we were on a short timeline to get the tour built in time for the first cruise ship that Spring. I was in charge of buying last minute hardware and supplies, cooking meals for the team, and continuing my work on the website, marketing, reservations, and creating a daily schedule.

Most people would assume that building a tour like that in the dead of winter would be a crazy idea, but the boggy, alpine microclimate included an annual deluge of rainfall and snow that made the wetlands impossible to deal with once the snow melted. We would never have been able to roll those heavy spools of steel cable over the soggy wetlands without destroying them and we would have crushed all the skunk cabbage and devil's club in the area. So, we realized that putting down some tracks in the snow and packing them down would be the least invasive way to get our gear into the depths of the temperate rainforest of the Tongass.

We loaded massive amounts of heavy gear into several sleds and hiked into the woods, pulling the sleds full of gear into the valley below. We set up a basecamp in the woods to use for the next six weeks of construction. Most of the gear was packed into storage containers to keep us from hauling it in and out each day. We took the climbing ropes and harnesses out with us at the end of each day to dry out overnight.

The days were a blur. We were so physically and mentally exhausted each night that we turned on the movie Step Into Liquid each night and fell asleep without talking. The imagery of that beautiful surfing movie carried me through those long days, but I don't think we made it to the end of the film until after the build was complete. Those were the earliest days of mail order DVDs, and we signed up for a plan and received that DVD in the mail in March. It wasn't until late September that we realized we still had the movie and returned it. We were getting our asses kicked so badly that we didn't even know what we were missing and that was probably a good thing.

One night after our tour construction was complete there was a full moon, so we hiked up the mountain through the snow until we reached the trees where we built our tour. It's hard to put into words the emotions that I felt looking up at the platforms and cables in the glow of moonlight that night. It was silent outside, and we didn't have to answer to anyone about anything. There was no construction noise. It was just the two of us marveling over what we accomplished together. We'd busted our asses for about two years planning for that moment, and it finally arrived. There was something synergistic about the two of us together. We were more than the sum of our parts. We were multiplicative, and we were moved to tears over what we were able to pull off in such a short time. We were overwhelmed with emotion and felt very connected with each other lying alone in the snow under the soft moonlight. We soaked in the magic of that moment together, and it was the last quiet moment we had for a while.

The next thing on the agenda was training. Our entire crew went through some extensive training together. We spent long days up in the trees zipping, rappelling, learning to tie knots and rescue each other from the middle of the cable. We had a lot of fun, but it was hard work. The hike into the woods in the snow each day alone was enough to wear out some people who were not properly conditioned for this kind of work.

Once training was complete, we offered to take some local family and friends out on the tour so we could all get some practice with the logistics. I will never forget the very first group of people we took out. It was cold and wet, and darkness crept in on us quickly as we zipped from one platform to the next. I could see every thought on the faces of our family and friends that day: fear, excitement, and finally relief when it was all over. I was the "Sending Guide" that day while Matt was the "Receiving Guide". The Receiving Guide was really the lead guide because they were the first one to zip to the next platform and assess the safety before giving their okay for the guests to fly across the line. Also, they were the primary person who would be in charge of any retrievals if a guest didn't make it all the way across the line.

My hands were frozen to the bone and soaking wet but I didn't wear any gloves on that first tour because I wanted to get everything right. Clipping each person into their pulley on the cable took a long time, and I had to do that on several ziplines. I didn't want to take the chance of getting a glove caught in the pulleys.

One of our family friends, Larry, was on the tour that day and he noticed that I wasn't wearing any gloves. The next night he showed up on the doorstep of the simple apartment we had recently moved into with a bag of several different types of gloves he bought from the store. "I wasn't sure which ones would work the best, so I got several kinds for you. You can just try them out until you find some that work. You need to wear gloves out there!" He was right. I thanked him sincerely and went inside to try them all on. We were so fortunate to have family and friends in town who really cared about us and our well-being.

Soon, the first ship arrived and we began one of the steepest learning curves of our lives. Starting that business was such a rollercoaster ride. One day we would be on top of the world and the next we felt hopeless. It was a wild ride that left us equal parts thrilled and exhausted.

Gil came to visit us, and we asked him if he would mind being in a photograph of our tour. We wanted to get a photo that captured the beautiful alpine scenery that surrounded the area. He happily offered to help us out with the photo but he was a little nervous about heights. Matt assured him that he would make sure he was safe. He placed a knotted rope behind the pulley to stop it from continuing to go down the line, and Gil carefully stepped off the platform onto the zipline cable. The knot brought Gil to a firm stop about eighty feet above the ground, just as they planned. He patiently allowed Matt to take a long series of photographs, then Matt told Gil he could remove the knot and he would glide to the next platform where Matt would meet him. He began to glide but came to an abrupt halt in the middle of the cable.

"The pulley is stuck on the rope. I can't get the rope out!" Gil yelled back to Matt.

"That's okay, I can just come out there and cut your lanyard and use a rope to lower you to the ground." Matt shouted back.

"No way am I letting you cut me down. We're gonna figure this out."

Eventually, Matt eased himself out onto the cable with Gil, carefully tying himself to the tree behind him so he wouldn't slide down the cable with Gil once he was free. When Matt reached Gil, he used his shears to cut the knotted rope that was stuck in the pulley. Eventually, he was able to cut the rope away from the pulley completely and Gil glided to the next platform. They had to work pretty hard to get that memorable picture, but it made for fun memories once it was over.

For the next five months of the Alaska tourism season, we worked twelve to seventeen-hour days. We met tourists at the cruise ships, drove the shuttle van, guided tours, sold photos and videos to the tourists, then drove them back to their ships. Late at night after we got home, we developed marketing strategies, created daily schedules for the following year and sent in applications to several cruise lines to sell our tours directly on their ships.

My favorite part about taking people ziplining through the Tongass rainforest wasn't the spectacular scenery or the thrill of flying through the air, it was truly watching the transformation of our guests. People would show up scared out of their minds. Lots of people who came on our tour were coerced by family members or friends and they had a fear of heights. There was such a warm fuzzy feeling when you were able to help others overcome their fears.

Almost every day, people told us "this was the best experience of my life". *Wow*. Those were powerful words and we received them with gratitude. We had most definitely found our edge with the business we'd built. One morning, an older woman showed up at the lodge to do our zipline tour. She was a local Juneau resident named Marjorie and she had big, black sunglasses on.

She asked me "Do you have a maximum age limit?"

I said "No, as long as you are physically able to do it and you have a spirit of adventure, we'd love to take you out!"

She replied, coyly "Good, because today is my 90th birthday."

It was such an honor to bring her out on the tour. We really had to prove ourselves that year. When we first opened, the only space we were offered was the small ticket office on the first floor of the lodge. There was no room for our guests or merchandise, so we were very limited with our capacity and sales.

Whenever we had a spare moment, we hiked the local mountain trails and stayed in remote forest service cabins. We met a wonderful group of friends and enjoyed the community of Juneau where people really cared about and looked out for one another. I felt so fortunate to make a group of girlfriends who were remarkable, accomplished women. We had a lot of fun together and they had an uncanny ability to keep me laughing, even on the hardest days. At first, we started a "Book Club", but quickly a couple of the girls confessed they had no interest in reading together. They just wanted to laugh and drink wine and that was fine by me.

In the middle of the summer, we decided we were due for a girl's night, but it wasn't going to be an ordinary girl's night. The plan was for us to take a float plane to a remote place called the Taku Glacier Lodge. Our brilliant friend Holly from our Book Club was in charge of the float plane tours that went out to the lodge, and she generously offered to coordinate the logistics for our group to make a special trip.

The Taku Lodge is a magical and sacred place with deep roots in our family. Matt's Grandparents once owned and lived at the Taku Lodge. What a special place it must have been for his mom and siblings to grow up. Matt's grandfather Gil often helped animals in distress. One time, he found a lost baby moose, and he nursed it back to health by feeding it milk in a bottle. They also took a seal in to help strengthen it back up, so it stayed in the bathtub. What an adventurous life they must have been living in that remote wilderness area!

The Lodge can only be reached by float plane or boat. It was built in the 1920s as a hunting and fishing lodge. In the 1930's an adventurous woman named Mary Joyce took over the lodge, and she raised and sold sled dogs all over the state of Alaska. She famously made a 1,000 mile, three month journey north to Fairbanks with her dogs, then opened the lodge as a tourist resort. Matt's family owned the lodge in the 1960s, and now it is owned by the Ward family who take great care of the Lodge and share this sacred place with tourists each summer while also offering a salmon bake overlooking some magnificent glaciers.

So, our girl's night involved flying to the Taku Glacier Lodge by float plane, then staying the night out there, and flying back the next morning. We brought provisions to share with the family who lived there and ran the tours of the lodge. They were very kind and welcoming to us that night, even though they must have been tired from a long day's work already. Matt's cousin Evan came by the lodge that evening and offered to take us out for a ride on his jet boat. We all jumped at the offer. We were taking in the sights of the glaciers and wildlife in the area, when we suddenly felt a huge thud as the boat came to a screeching halt.

We hit a sandbar, and our friend Mariah flew into the front of the boat and hit her head on the piece of glacier ice we just harvested. She sat up after a moment and told us she cut her head.

Holly, the quick-witted master of comedic timing, quickly remarked "Why does it always have to be about you?"

Knowing that she wasn't injured badly, we all erupted into laughter. That's just what we needed in that moment to cut the tension. We double-checked on her to make sure she was okay. Then, it dawned on us that we were stuck and it was getting late. It was still light outside, but there was not a soul in sight. Evan had a chainsaw wench, and he went into the water to secure one end in the sandbar and we connected the cable to the chainsaw that I was holding. Then, the girls held my legs in the boat to keep me from being pulled out. We tried and tried to pull the boat loose with the wench, but we couldn't get it to move. Finally, Mike from the Lodge heard we were stuck out there, and he came to the rescue in another boat and helped us get free of the sandbar. We made our way back to the lodge and slept in a nearby cabin. That was most definitely a girl's night to remember!

When we flew back to Juneau, I told Matt about our adventures and I could tell he was a little envious. He loved experiences like that, and it got us thinking that we would love to have a boat of our own to explore the incredible waters of Southeast Alaska. The problem was that we didn't have the money for a boat. We looked and looked and finally we found her. She was an old Bayliner Trophy from the 1980s. She needed some work, but the price was right at less than five thousand dollars. There was a small inflatable zodiac that came with the boat that offered some comfort in case the boat had problems.

The fan belt on the boat needed to be replaced, so there was a loud screeching noise that could be heard for miles around us whenever we went out on the boat. We donned her the "Mile Away" because you could hear us coming from miles away. We had great times on that little boat. Matt's Uncle Al taught us how to troll for salmon, so we spent most of our spare time fishing for salmon and throwing in crab pots.

Through a major stroke of beginner's luck, the first salmon that I ever caught was a white king salmon. The meat of a wild Alaska king salmon is typically a vivid red color. Some king salmon – about one in twenty – have white meat due to an inability to process the pigments in their food. Although these white kings have long been coveted by Alaskans, the pale meat typically fetched a lower price from fish buyers and was considered commercially less desirable. But now white kings are making a splash in the commercial market as people have realized white king's flavor is more delectable than their more common cousin. The tide has turned and now it is often marketed as "ivory king," yielding a higher price.

When I reeled in the salmon, I had no idea it was a white king. It wasn't until we filleted it later that day, that we could tell the difference. We naively made sashimi with the salmon that night. We enjoyed every bite of it but later learned that raw fish should normally be flash frozen to destroy any parasites in the fish before eating it.

Later that summer, the Mile Away blew a head gasket while our friends Buzz and Drew were visiting us from Los Angeles. Thank goodness we had a spare motor, a kicker, on hand for just that situation. We were a little embarrassed about our old boat breaking down, and we had to cruise back quite a long way through the Gastineau Channel before we could make it to the marina where we kept the boat docked. We had to pass the huge cruise ships where people were drinking wine from their balconies and looking down on us in our little boat. We decided to troll for salmon because at least that gave us something to do and made us look like we intended to go that slowly.

Since the boat was out of commission for a while, we decided to go out and check our crab pots in the dinghy. We'd never seen anyone else using a dinghy and oars to check their crab pots, but that wasn't going to stop us. About halfway to our destination, we noticed a couple kids on the shore laughing really hard.

We hollered over "Just what is so funny?"

They kept laughing and finally managed to say "You're paddling that raft out to check your crab pots? That's so funny!"

Yeah, real funny kids. We didn't care what anyone thought of us. We were so determined to live life to the fullest and enjoy each moment. The crab tasted extra sweet that night.

(Left:) Rachel 2004. (Right:) Matt 2006.

(Left:) Me with a white king salmon. (Right:) Trolling for salmon on the Mile-Away.

(Left:) Photo shoot of Matt's brother Gil. (Right:) Matt digging out of the snow.

Whatever our souls are made of, his and mine are the same. ~ Emily Bronte

Heart of Gold

At the end of our first season running zipline tours in Alaska, we planned to get married at the end of September. We completely underestimated what it would take to break down the tour for the winter and move all of our business belongings out of the ski lodge so they could prepare for their winter season. Our last tour was on a Tuesday, and we flew to Zihuatanejo, Mexico for our small destination wedding two days later. It was a nearly impossible challenge, but somehow we managed to pull it off and catch our flight.

We chose Zihuatanejo for our wedding destination because we remembered it as the peaceful fishing village shown at the end of the movie Shawshank Redemption. It seemed like the perfect little oasis for us to share such a special moment with our family and friends.

Pretty much my whole life before I met Matt, I thought I would never get married. It was difficult to imagine a normal wedding since my parents were divorced, and they didn't have a very amicable relationship. I couldn't envision how that would work out comfortably for all of us, but we decided to do something very unconventional. We didn't plan any of the details of the wedding. We simply felt that we loved each other and the people who cared about us most would be there to support us and share in the celebration of our love.

It was truly heart-warming to find out that Mom and Dad and his lovely wife Eva would all be coming to the wedding, and they really didn't bring any drama into the weekend whatsoever. I'm sure it must have been difficult for Mom to see her ex-husband with his current wife, especially because her husband John, my step dad, couldn't make it to the wedding. I was sad that he couldn't make it because I knew Mom could use his support with the unique dynamic, but I understood it wasn't possible due to work and financial constraints.

About fifty of our closest family and friends joined us for a beachside ceremony and reception in Zihuatanejo, and it was a magical, memorable experience for all of us. We truly didn't plan any details of the wedding in advance, so when we showed up to our little boutique hotel, where everyone would be staying and the ceremony would be taking place, we were blown away by the beauty of it all. It felt like the perfect little spot to gather with our loved ones for this momentous occasion. The woman assigned to help us with our wedding greeted us with a glass of fresh juice, and showed us several photos. We looked over them and quickly chose the look that we liked the best. We went with simple white tablecloths, white candles and bright orange flowers from the local nursery. We went to the nursery and picked out the flowers ourselves later that day. The setting was already so perfect that we didn't need much in the way of adornment. We did, however, agree on having the mariachis play after our ceremony. Growing up in San Antonio for many years, I had a nostalgic feeling about mariachis, and it seemed like the perfect nod to my roots.

Matt and I decided against having a "wedding party" comprised of bridesmaids and groomsmen. It felt as though we would be somehow ranking or valuing some people as more important than others. We asked Matt's Mom to walk him down the aisle and my Mom to walk me down the aisle. Again, it wasn't very conventional, but Mom busted her tail raising me on her own for most of my life and I felt that it was only right that she would be the one to walk me down the aisle. I loved my dad very much and I wanted him to be a meaningful part of the ceremony, so I asked him if he would play a couple of songs during the ceremony and he very lovingly agreed to do it. He chose the perfect songs, and my heart warmed watching him stand up there in his crisp white linen shirt with his harmonica strapped around his neck, and his guitar around his shoulders. The highlight for us was when he played *Heart of Gold* by Neil Young. It felt so perfect for that moment, and he did a beautiful job.

Matt and I were both pretty nervous and a little sweaty from the sweltering heat. As we looked at one another and listened to the words taken as excerpts from Khalil Gibran's The Profit, we felt the enormity of the moment like we were covered in a honey bucket of love.

"Love one another, but make not a bond of love, Let it rather be a moving sea between the shores of your souls." We exchanged rings and we had the words "In the Fog" engraved inside of Matt's ring as a nod to the unlikely way we met that day in the fog on a breast cancer event surrounded by thousands of women.

Once the ceremony was over, we popped open the champagne to share with everyone and we all made our way down to the beach for the reception. We dined on fresh tuna and wine then we made our way to each table to talk to our guests. A couple people stood up to give speeches, and they were just the right fit for the occasion. My bestie Tara stood up and shared her thoughts about our many years of friendship and travels to far flung countries together. She spoke of our shared love for adventure and how we were Soul Sisters, then she said that Matt was the perfect match for my adventurous spirit and we all toasted.

Then, Matt's dad stood up and gave an awesome, unexpected speech about the "test" he and his dad put me through in the Wrangell St Elias mountains when Matt and I first met. *Yes!* I had always told Matt I felt the moose heart, barbecued beaver, and sleeping in a snow shelter were all a part of a test, but Matt didn't believe it. Now, his dad announced it to the crowd and everyone soaked up the unique nature of the story. He talked about the importance of tolerance and his words really resonated with us. What a phenomenal feeling we had that night to be surrounded by the people we cared about so much while we made this commitment to each other. We ended the night by having our loved ones write their wishes for us on paper lanterns, then we all lit them and sent them up into the sky.

The next morning, the concierge at the hotel showed us the front page of the newspaper. The picture captured the lanterns floating into the sky, but they translated the caption for us, and it said "UFO Sightings". We laughed for a long time, then we took some mopeds to a remote surfing beach and relaxed a bit with our family and friends.

We returned home to Alaska from our wedding and were quickly thrust out of our newlywed bliss. We crunched some numbers and realized we were broke. We had just enough money in the bank to pay back all the loans we received to start the business and cover our taxes, but we only had a few hundred dollars left after that. The tourism season was over, so that meant we wouldn't have any more earnings until the following summer.

We came to the conclusion that we needed to find some seasonal work. We called some of our friends who worked on breast cancer events and asked if we could work on their Tent Crew for a few events. We really needed the money to survive at that point. We also agreed to do a couple of events helping to train the new team who would be managing the educational breast cancer exhibit tour that Matt and I previously managed.

After a couple of months of work, Tara mentioned that she was going to the Caribbean to meet her boyfriend there who was sailing over from Portugal. We used airline miles to book our flights to the Caribbean. We ended up in St John in the Virgin Islands. As usual, we didn't do any research in advance, so we landed there and realized most of the accommodations on the island were expensive hotels we couldn't afford. We really only had a tiny amount of money for that trip and the main plan was to meet Tara and her boyfriend to sail around the Caribbean for a few days on her boyfriend's sixty foot catamaran. Before we met up with them, we had a few weeks to explore, so we just had to figure out how to make it work financially. We bought some used camping gear and camped in Cinnamon Bay on St John, then we took the ferry to Jost Van Dyke, Virgin Gorda and Tortola, camping there as well. The mosquitoes and sand fleas pretty much destroyed us in the tent each night, but during the day we swam in the impossibly clear blue waters, snorkeled among some beautiful coral reefs and hiked to remote beaches for picnics.

After a couple weeks in the BVIs, we decided to hop on a ferry to Puerto Rico. We ended up in Fajardo, where some people we met on the ferry had told us to check out the bioluminescent waters. We decided to do the tour and stay there that night after agreeing to share a room with some other travelers so we could afford to make it happen. That night we took kayaks out on the water and every time I put the oars in the water, the water turned bright neon blue. We saw glowing fish swim by and we jumped in the water to go for a swim. It was a truly exhilarating experience but it wasn't quite the same as the trip our roommate was having. He decided to take some mushrooms that night and he was in a whole different world. When we went back to our room that night, he talked for hours about the bioluminescence and we finally faded off to sleep in the middle of his stories.

The next day, we took a ferry to the island of Vieques. On our first night there, we met a really sweet couple who owned a restaurant and B&B called Bananas. They took us under their wings and offered to take us snorkeling around the island. They picked us up in their jeep and we had an invigorating day snorkeling with them.

We couldn't find a good camping option at the time and we were feeling the need for a real shower, so we approached a basic B&B and asked if we could work in exchange for a room. They agreed and we were so excited. We went into the room, and it felt like we hit the lottery. There was nothing special about that room, but it had walls and a bathroom with a shower and a toilet. Those were luxury items we hadn't seen on that trip.

The next morning, we met the owner of the inn to see what work we could do for them. The woman told us we would be scraping paint off the concrete floors of her huge outdoor patio. We were on our knees scraping paint for the entire day. Several young couples walked by and offered us a ride to the beach, but we told them we had committed to do that work. We never imagined how long and hard the work would be but we finished it. Then, we left there that evening with aching backs and knees.

Our new friends invited us to their personal home for Thanksgiving. They had a picturesque house overlooking the ocean with a swimming pool. It felt like a tropical paradise, and we enjoyed long conversations with them about how they met and traveled around together before making the move to Vieques. That night, their daughter and her boyfriend also joined us for dinner and her boyfriend proposed to her, so it was a very special evening that will be forever in our memories. We had bacon wrapped dates, gourmet cheese and delectable wine. There was so much to be thankful for, but we were missing our family and friends.

Soon after that, we left to meet Tara and her boyfriend for the sailing adventure. The three of us were excited at the novel adventure of sailing in the open seas, but her boyfriend arrived feeling exhausted and needing to do some repairs on his boat. Also, there was bad weather in the forecast, and we needed to buy provisions, so we waited a few days before it was safe to set sail. Since none of us were experienced sailors, he had to give us a quick lesson. Then, we took turns through the night sailing among those choppy waters. To him, the seas probably seemed fairly normal, but to us it was a nail-biting experience. Large waves crashed against the boat through the night, and we felt a bit seasick and concerned about the conditions. A batton on the sail broke, and we had to help him repair it. We were concerned that if he went out to make the repair and went overboard, none of us would be knowledgeable enough to sail the boat on our own.

So, Matt offered to inch out onto the bowsprit hanging beyond the pulpit while Tara's boyfriend climbed up the mast to repair the batton. Matt laid out over the front of the boat as we went over some pretty big waves. It was a harrowing experience for me. When we made it to our final destination, we had a short time to do some snorkeling, then Matt and I needed to get back to Tortola for our flight home. We took the dinghy off the sailboat, jumped in, and raced over to the island and got totally soaked as our bodies slammed down with the crash of each wave. It was an intense end to the trip, but for the thrill-seekers inside of us, it was all that we could have hoped for and more.

(Left): Our parents (Matt's on left, Rachel's on right). (Right): Mariachis.

(Left): Tara, Me, Megan. (Right): Dad playing guitar

(Left): Releasing a sky lantern. (Right): Matt repairing the bowsprit.

The women whom I love and admire for their strength and grace did not get that way because shit worked out. They got that way because shit went wrong, and they handled it. ~Elizabeth Gilbert

Without a Paddle

We returned to Alaska to prepare for the next tourist season, and we decided to add two ziplines to the tour as well as a suspension bridge. We had no money for these improvements, but felt they were necessary, and we had promised our new cruise ship partners that these elements would be a part of the tour. We were determined to keep that promise, so we took out another loan.

Our Aunt and Uncle had some sweet neighbors who had some space available in their basement, and they generously offered it to us for a while until our next house sitting gig was available. There wasn't a kitchen in the basement but there was a coffee pot that also worked well for boiling water for ramen noodles. We were surviving on ramen and holding on by the seats of our pants. Each night before we went to sleep in our twin beds, we would say three things we were grateful for and it helped lift our spirits a little. I know we were supposed to find beauty in the smallest things like a flower or a beautiful sunset, but we kind of rotated through the same checklist each night. Our health, our family and our friends. It was hard to move beyond those things because our minds were so full of to-do items that needed to happen before the season began in a couple months.

Our builder was flying in the next day, so we woke up early and headed up to the mountain to prepare the area for construction. When we came down from the mountain that day, we were bone-tired but needed to get some gas in our tiny old pick-up. After we filled the tank with gas, we went into the station to pay. Matt said he was craving chili, so we grabbed two cans of it and located the stash of paper bowls and plastic ware that we had discovered a couple of weeks before. We pulled out our can opener, poured the chili into our bowls and heated them up in the microwave. This wasn't our first rodeo. We had done this a couple of times before. Chili in a can wasn't my favorite delicacy but it was what we could afford financially and time-wise.

The gas station attendant, who I am fairly confident was a meth addict, walked over to us and said "Look, I'm onto you guys. I know you've done this before, but can you try to at least clean up your mess this time?"

I was mortified. Those words sank down like weights to the ocean-bottom of my soul. I had no idea we had left a mess before, and I was beyond humiliated to have the gas station attendant take notice of this and reprimand us about it. I felt sure he thought we were homeless thugs who frequented this gas station to heat up our dinner and didn't even have the decency to properly clean up after ourselves (that wasn't far from the truth, I guess). He was a better person than I was in that moment. *How could I have judged him?* All of the shame and fear that I was feeling was being broadcast out for the world to see. My freak flag was flying, but I hadn't given permission for it and I wasn't prepared. I was so humiliated and unearthed. I felt sure that was the lowest moment of my life.

Our builder, Todd, arrived the next afternoon, and he asked us to meet up with him that night to chat about a game plan. We met him at the Alaskan Hotel & Bar where he was staying. We bought him a beer, and talked for a while then Todd challenged me to a game of Galaga.

I asked him what the wager was going to be and he said "The suspension bridge".

The color drained from my face as I looked up to see if he was serious. "What do you mean?" I asked.

He said "If you win, I'll build you the suspension bridge for free."

Matt, had a huge grin on his face, his eyes lit up with excitement. He always believed in me more than I believed in myself.

"What do you win?" I asked nervously.

"We'll just keep the same terms we agreed on for payment of the bridge".

He was offering a wager I couldn't refuse but I still felt the weight of the offer and knew it was one I couldn't afford to lose. "I'm stacking what you're chopping. Let's do this."

I sat down on my side and Todd took his place across from me. The game began and I was off to a pretty strong start, but I made the mistake of talking a little trash and karma quickly took me down. He beat me heartily, and I was glad it wasn't close because my heart couldn't have taken it. I think he would have honored that bet if I'd won, so it was a bit tragic that I lost, but I got over it.

Before we knew it the first cruise ship arrived. Our second season of running tours arrived, and we expected things to be easier with some experience under our belts. Unfortunately, we were just more aware of what needed to happen, so we constantly felt behind. It felt like drinking water from a fire hose for five months straight.

The good news was that we had more guests come on our tour the second year. The bad news was that we had a lot of adjustments to make to bring our tour up to the high standards it would take to sustain ourselves. We asked if it would be possible to move into a more spacious, modern area of the ski lodge upstairs. We were crammed in a small ticket office in the basement the first year, and there wasn't any room for selling merchandise or showing our guests photos from their tour.

We repainted the entire upstairs area of the ski lodge inside, and we remodeled everything with couches and tables from our apartment. It was a second-hand, boho vibe, but it worked. We put a flat screen TV in the room, and we played videos and photos from the zipline tour in the rainforest for our guests when they got back to the lodge. We eventually got a seasonal beer and wine license, so we were able to offer our guests a local Alaskan beer to enjoy while they watched the memories of their experience flash on the TV screen. This really improved our guest experience and the reviews of our tour online reflected that.

We were finally getting in a rhythm and catching up on work enough that we were going to be able to enjoy a couple of days off. Megan flew in from the lower 48 with her husband Brian. They were two of our favorite people and we wanted to do something different with them. I researched permits for Pack Creek on Admiralty Island. The native people call it "Kootznoowoo" or "Fortress of the Bears." This remote island is a short float plane ride from Juneau and it has around 1,500 brown bears (more than all of the lower 48 bear populations combined).

We had to charter a float plane to take us there, then we had to borrow some kayaks and bring camping gear. There were a lot of logistics to cover but that was our wheelhouse. We got everything organized, and we were fortunate enough to have weather that allowed us to fly over on a rare stretch of two days off. We had so much fun hiking through the woods on the island and watching bears with their cubs feeding on salmon. The bears didn't really care about us much because their food supply was so plentiful. The park only allows twenty four people to visit the area each day and a permit is required, so it's not an experience that most people have access to when they go to Alaska.

When we got back to Juneau our friends went ice climbing while we worked, then we took them out on the Mile-Away that evening for some whale watching. We had so much fun on that old boat enjoying our own time with mother nature after all the tourists had left for the day. We were so grateful for that quiet time at the end of a long day. Brian had cut his head that day in an ice cave. The cut continued to bleed, so after our whale watching they went to the hospital so Brian could get stitches. Thankfully, he was okay and I guess it just gave him another story to remember from his trip to Alaska.

At the end of the summer season, we offered free tours to the Big Brothers & Big Sisters program and a couple of other local charity organizations. Then, we offered half-price tours to the local community during a Blueberry Festival where people would hike around the mountain picking blueberries and listening to local music. It was the least we could do to give back to the community after the season ended.

We asked our good friend Joanie, who owned a popular, whimsical bakery and coffee shop named Paradise, if we could make dinner for our staff in her adorably-outfitted space. She was all for it, so we made Italian food and lit candles, and drank wine, and shared stories from our season. We thanked our staff and gave them gifts and funny awards. It was a great time to reflect on everything. We capped the night off by walking outside to the dock that was above the Gastineau Channel.

Spontaneously, the entire crew decided to jump into the ocean in our clothes. It took a little convincing to get a few of our guides to jump, but we all agreed we would only do it if everyone jumped together. As I hit the water, I felt as though my heart instantly froze and seized in my chest. My chest was tightening and I felt like I couldn't breathe. I looked for Matt and he pointed at the swim ladder nearby. I swam faster than ever before, I barely remember stepping out of the water. I was sure that I was experiencing hypothermia and it was only the end of September. I was fine, but that swim put me in check a little.

Matt and I still had one vehicle between us, and it was the old beater pick-up truck that we affectionately named "Little Engine". It served us well and we didn't have the money to get another car. Once the summer season was over, the Ski Area Manager gave us season passes. One day I slid off the road into a ditch while driving up the mountain to go skiing. Thankfully, our friend Bryan was coming down the mountain, and he pulled my truck out of the ditch with his truck and a tow-strap. I'm not sure how we would've made it without the help from our friends and community. Oftentimes, it really felt like the wheels were coming off in many aspects of our life.

That winter, we started a consulting business where we flew around the country helping other people start their own zipline tours while ours was closed for the winter. Our third year of running tours was a turning point for us. After grinding so hard for the first two years, we grew our business substantially to a level that allowed us to hire an experienced supervisor who could oversee the daily operations on a regular basis. This enabled us to tend to things like marketing and email communications, business development, scheduling and community involvement during the day, instead of being in the constant grind. It felt like we could finally breathe a bit and focus on growing our business and improving our tour experience.

That summer, we also had a unique opportunity to plan a special trip with our good friends Tisha and Jeremy. Matt and I had taken a day trip out on a boat to Tracy Arm at the end of the previous summer. Two photographers brought their own kayak on the boat and had the boat captain drop it over the edge so they could kayak around the glacier. As soon as I saw them do that, I knew that was what we had to do.

We went about making plans for the four of us to sail out to Tracy Arm, drop two kayaks overboard that we could crawl into and load our gear up for an overnight camping trip. We founds maps of the area and, with some research, found out there was one safe camping area that was high enough that it was above the tide line and also less likely to be reached by bears.

We packed plenty of good food and every little gadget we could possibly need that would fit into a kayak. When we were reviewing all of our gear, I suggested to Matt that we should bring flares and he laughed at me. He thought it was silly and we wouldn't have a need for them, but I convinced him to bring them anyway. We had some in our boat, so I grabbed them and we crammed them into our dry bag. There was no room for anything else by that point.

On the morning of our trip we met our friends at the office where the boat tour groups were gathered. Our spirits were high as we drank coffee and noticed there were some sucker holes in the sky. Locals call them sucker holes because you are a sucker if you think that little spot of blue in the sky means the clouds are going to clear because that rarely happens in Southeast Alaska.

Our journey to Tracy Arm took a few hours. Less than an hour into the trip, we realized that somehow our group had forgotten to pack the kayak paddles onto the boat! We told the boat captain about it, and he said they had some snow shovels onboard we could use for paddles but we all agreed that wouldn't be the safest option. We had rented a satellite phone for this trip because we would be camping in a very remote location with no other people anywhere around for miles. If one of us flipped our kayak or a bear approached us, we needed a way to call for help or the consequences could be fatal. We used it to call our friend Arne who was a pilot and owned a local fly-fishing business. He knew the area where we were going very well.

We agreed to split the cost of flying a plane out to drop the paddles to us so that we could enjoy the rest of our trip. That was a $500 trip he made that day, but it was so worth it for those memories that will last a lifetime. Just as Arne was flying overhead, our boat captain radioed another nearby boat and asked to borrow some kayak paddles they had onboard. We pulled up to their boat and they gave us the paddles. We called off the plane, so he didn't have to land, but we still had to pay for that flight. Back-country trips are tricky to plan because any item that is missing from your list can truly put your life in peril.

The boat finally pulled up to the area near the glacier where we would be camping and they lowered the kayaks into the water for us. Now we had to make our way down to the kayaks and try not to slip or fall while getting in and putting our gear inside. I don't like having an audience, so it was stressful for me to do all of this with the entire crowd of passengers lined up on the side of the boat watching us in awe. We were far from experts at kayaking and this could go wrong so easily. Thankfully, the four of us loaded into our kayaks without too much trouble and we were off.

It felt magical to be kayaking through such pristine emerald colored waters surrounded by high rock walls on both sides. We paddled around for a while, then we decided to set up camp. We pulled our boats up onto the steep rock wall and fastened them, then we pulled out our tents, sleeping bags, and provisions for the night. Once we set everything up, we decided to take the kayaks out to the glacier. We joked that we felt like we were floating around in a giant margarita.

There were hundreds of small icebergs surrounding us as we paddled towards the glacier. Seals were pupping, and we took photos of them as they sunbathed on the ice. As we paddled closer to the glacier, it began calving, so we sat in our kayaks and watched in awe as huge, centuries-old shelves of ice cracked and fell magnificently into the water in front of us. We cautiously monitored the swell of the water as it rose in front of us and paddled directly into it so we didn't end up broadside. The last thing we wanted was be flipped over by a rogue wave. We were basically kayak-surfing the swell from this fantastic, calving glacier and I was giddy from the beauty of it all.

Once we all had our fill at the glacier, we paddled back towards our campsite. Giant sculptures of ice were jutting out from the water and we kayaked under and through some of them, marvelling at the wonder of it all. That night we made a delicious dinner and took in the stunning landscape that surrounded us. I slept hard that night after a long day in the sun.

The next morning, we packed up camp. We were told to paddle out for a couple of hours to the meeting spot where the boat was going to pick us up. We didn't want to be late, so we got an early start. We paddled into the middle of the channel where it was probably only a couple of hundred feet between the rock walls on either side. They told us to wait there and wave our paddles because it was the easiest place to find us. We laughed and joked around until we saw the boat coming. We were very obvious in our red and yellow kayaks and brightly colored rain jackets.

We waved our paddles overhead as they suggested, but the large boat full of passengers went around us and kept going. They were leaving the area to go back to Juneau, and they drove on at full speed without looking back at us. We were yelling and waving our paddles but it didn't help. "How could they have possibly missed us?" I asked, defeated. Floating at sea, forgotten, I felt a familiar feeling rise up as my chest tightened. I was all too familiar with those feelings of being left behind, and I felt responsible for putting us in that situation. It was my fault for coming up with this crazy idea, and now it was going to be my fault when we all died of starvation. Finally, Matt broke the silence and suggested we should stay there in case there was another boat. It never occurred to me that another boat might be coming by that day.

After about thirty minutes, another boat went by and we waved our paddles in front of them, but the same thing happened. They drove around us and sped away.

"Grab the flares, Matt!" I yelled out of desperation.

Matt dug for the flares and managed to locate them fairly quickly. He pulled the trigger and fired one flare above the boat. It made an arc in the sky and the light and smoke came down in front of where the boat was headed. The boat immediately slowed down. He had one chance to get it right, and he shot it perfectly. The boat slowly turned around and came over to us. All of the passengers on board were wide-eyed and took photos of us as we talked to the crew on the boat. The guests onboard thought they were witnessing a life or death rescue of some kind and they were fascinated. We explained that the boat we were supposed to catch left us and there wouldn't be any other boats coming by that day. We didn't have any more food provisions and we had to work the next day. We had no other option. We needed to climb aboard that boat. So, the crew helped us climb up and pull our kayaks and gear out of the water. The guests on board clapped when we came inside and I was slightly embarrassed, but my feelings of gratitude won over. I was so happy to be safe and heading back home to our warm apartment that night with memories that I would reflect on for years to come.

(Left):Me & Matt on our suspension bridge, Juneau, AK. (Right): Brown bear,, AK

Kayaking between the glaciers. Tracy Arm Fjord. Photo by Jeremy Geiser

My mission in life is not merely to survive but to thrive and to do so with some passion, some compassion, some humor, and some style. ~Maya Angelou

Home Sweet Home

The economy was in a free-fall, and we weren't sure what would be in store for our small tourism business the following summer. We had a lot of work to do that winter, but we saved up enough for a trip to visit my family in Switzerland, and we planned to do a little more exploring with a side trip to Turkey, Spain and Morocco. We flew into Zurich first and visited my dad, step-mom, and half-sisters and brother. At the end of each day, Dad played music with his friend Jimmy in the music room. I really enjoyed that time with my family in Switzerland. It's always good to see Dad, and Eva and I have developed such a lovely, warm relationship. I feel so fortunate to have her as a second Mom. But I especially treasured my time with my siblings because they were growing up so quickly, and they changed so much between our visits. We enjoyed our time together, then we took a flight to Istanbul. We were entranced by the beautiful city. We stayed in a small hotel called Empress Zoe and explored the incredible mosques and bazaars, enjoying beautiful meals. Then, we made our way to Cappadocia, a region in central Turkey known for its fairy chimneys tall cone shaped rock formations. The area is also known for Bronze Age homes carved into valley walls by cave dwellers. It's a whimsical place, and we stayed there for several days soaking up the uniqueness of it all.

Next, we made our way to southern Spain where we enjoyed delicious tapas and walked around the cities exploring the museums and architecture. Then, we decided to take a boat from Tarifa, Spain over to northern Africa. Morocco was stunning with its colorful medinas and souks. We took a train through the country and explored Marrakech, Casablanca, Fez, Chefchaoen, and the Atlas Mountains. We even took an overnight camel trek through the Saharan desert near the Algerian border. We booked by payphone and were told a man named Hassan would meet us in Merzouga off the overnight bus. We had to use fake names on the bus - apparently, sometimes people hear other people's names being mentioned on the bus, then use those names to get on the camel tour. We decided we would be Maggie and Jackson. Those were the names of two of our friends' dogs from Alaska.

Hassan had a password for us so we'd know he was the correct guide. It was "Forty".

When we arrived in Merzouga in the dark, a man came up to us and said "Are you Rachel & Matt?"

I said "Yes, do you have a password for us?"

He replied "I am Hassan. Forty".

This whole experience was very mysterious and exciting for us but we wondered what kind of trickery was going on in this area. Hassan loaded us into the back seat of a pink truck, another man got into the passenger seat, they turned up the Arabic music and they sped through the desert for about an hour. They brought us to a small hotel, didn't say a single word to us, opened the door to a room and pointed inside. We walked into the room and closed the door.

This wasn't the tour we'd agreed upon. There was no mention of a hotel. It was actually pretty nice, but we were a little concerned for our safety. Finally, we wandered out to the front desk area and found a nice woman who spoke a little English.

I said "Can you please tell us why we are here?" I realized after I said that how scared our parents would have been if they had known what was happening.

She replied "You need to rest".

That was all she said. It began to sink in. We had taken an overnight bus and we hadn't slept much. We went back to our room and slept cautiously while holding our backpacks. We woke up to the sound of loud knocks on the door. I was terrified. Matt asked who it was and the man said "Hassan". He slowly opened the door and Hassan motioned for us to follow him. We climbed into his truck again and we stopped at a remote place in the desert where some children played music for us. They were all dressed in white sheets. The music was unbelievable and we enjoyed the experience, but we were still very confused because this wasn't what we signed up for. After the music was over, Hassan loaded us back into his truck, drove a little further, then stopped on the side of the road in the middle of the desert where two men were standing with camels. They were supposed to be our guides, but we quickly learned that they didn't speak any English.

The next twenty four hours were a bit of a comedy routine. We acted things out in interpretive dance and eventually someone would understand what we were saying. About halfway through our camel trek out to the remote desert spot where we would eventually sleep that night, Matt decided he had enough of his camel. He was paranoid that he was too big for it and he was convinced his camel didn't like him very much. I was laughing so hard.

"Why don't you think he likes you?" I asked.

"Because he keeps groaning and kneeling down. I would rather walk." Matt replied, his mind made up.

"Okay, whatever makes you happy" I said as my camel and I sauntered on happily through the desert.

We arrived at a canvas tent in the desert that night, and our guides made us a delicious tagine and mint tea and wrapped turbans around our heads. They then pointed at us and said "Ber-ber" (what they called local native Arabs) and erupted into fits of laughter. We had a great time, but it was extremely odd that they didn't speak any English. When I woke up the next morning, my stomach was hurting pretty badly. There was no toilet, and we had limited toilet paper. The game of charades I had to play to convey to them what was going on was epic. Finally, it seemed they were stacking what I was chopping, and they gathered things up so we could make our way back to town. When we arrived, they drove us to a small outdoor spice market and Hassan walked us up to a table and spoke to a child who was working there. The child poured some brown powder into my hand, and I stood there with a quizzical look on my face. Hassan and the boy both put their hands to their mouths as if to say "eat it". So I did. I'm pretty sure I swallowed about three tablespoons of it, but I was grateful it had a familiar taste. It was cumin, and it did the trick.

Shortly after our jaunt in the Saharan Desert, work beckoned so we flew home to prepare for the tourism season. We revamped our website and made a real effort to tell our story about how we started the business. One thing we realized with time is that our story was what set us apart from the competition. In the beginning, we felt intimidated by other companies who had more money and resources than we did.

Over time, we realized that the one thing we had was a unique, boot-strapping story, so we re-vamped our marketing strategy and focused on a simple, authentic portrayal of who we are and how we built the business. It really seemed to help us find customers during a difficult financial time. Our tour was also less expensive than many others, so that helped a bit, too. One day that Spring, before the first cruise ship arrived, I was on my laptop and saw an announcement for a small business contest. They asked business owners to submit an essay explaining how their small business did creative marketing to make them stand out. So, I wrote an essay really quickly and forgot about it. I didn't even bother mentioning it to Matt because I never imagined anything would come of it.

I was completely shocked in September when I got a call from NBC saying that our company was a finalist in the competition. Somehow, we lucked out and we were chosen as the winners of the Cool Runnings Contest for Coolest Small Business in America. NBC flew a crew out to run a piece on our business and the creative (low-cost) marketing strategies we were using to get the word out about our business in a tight economy. We were honored by the award, but what we truly enjoyed the most was making lifetime friends with a few of the crew members that came out to film the video about our company, especially Shawna and Tony. They were so insightful and fun and it was like the cherry on top of a good season for us that year.

We finally rented a nice apartment in downtown Juneau and we bought a second car. It was a used station wagon but it offered us so much freedom. We worked different schedules and we needed to be in different places at different times. Over the first few years, we just hopped in one of the shuttles if we needed a ride up the mountain to work or back down at the end of the day. Those shuttles saved us for a long time, but it was such a treat to have a second car so we could actually ride to work in privacy and peace instead of being surrounded by customers all the time.

Commercial Zipline Tours didn't have approved building and operating standards with which to regulate the safety of the industry in the early years of development. So, I volunteered as the only female on an international Zipline/Canopy Tour Committee with five men. We spent countless hours working together to draft the initial building and operations standards for the industry.

After that summer tour season was over, we had to buy another shuttle van. We got a good deal on a used one from the company I worked for during my trek-leading days. We flew to LA to pick it up and decided to take the seats out and put them into storage. We went on a road-trip through Utah and California exploring the National Parks. We got permits to hike the Subway in Zion and we went mountain biking in Moab. We camped in Arches National Park, and we covered miles through Canyonlands. At the end of this trip, we decided that we would explore some small towns in northern California and Oregon to see if we could find a place that resonated with us to spend the winters during our off season. When we first pulled into Bend, Oregon, we knew we'd found our town. We spent some time there hiking and exploring the mountains and lakes, then we found our dog, Z. Well, she found us. Some people advertised that they wanted to give her up because she was a runt. They had cut her tail off, and they were disappointed that she wasn't a full size German Short-Haired Pointer. To us, she was perfect. She wasn't at all what we had in mind when we were planning to get a dog, but she was the first dog we saw and with one look, we knew that we would be taking her with us.

We decided to look at houses the next day. Since the housing market was suffering from the economic fall-out from the past year, there were some good deals out there. We found the perfect little first home for us, and we decided to make an offer. We didn't think it would be accepted, so we were heading out of town to Portland when we got the call that our offer was accepted! We pulled over and got out of the car. We didn't care what the people thought as they drove by while we embraced on the side of the road. We were going to be home owners! It took us a while to get to that point, but that made the accomplishment so much sweeter. We turned around and went back to Bend to sign the papers. We spent a little time nesting after the house closed, but the tourism season in Alaska was approaching.

I flew with our dog Z (short for Zihuatanejo where we were married) to Juneau while Matt visited with his friend Seth in Washington before he had to put the van on the barge to Alaska. When I landed, I met some friends for a snowy hike with our dogs. The other dog that went on the hike that day was Maggie, one of my favorite dogs on the planet who I pretended to be on the bus in Morocco. I was so excited to expose Z to her wonderful new home with great hiking trails abound. About a mile into our hike, I heard her squeal and when I walked up to her, I saw that her face was covered in quills. My friends had experience with getting porcupine quills out of their dog, so they got some pliers and helped me try to remove all of them. Unfortunately, Z wasn't having it. She was squealing so much and pulling away from us, there were just too many quills. I had to call the vet who did emergency surgery that weekend to remove the quills. What a first day in Alaska that must have been for sweet little Z.

When the tour season began that year, I decided that I wanted to use our business to help others in a more meaningful way. We donated tours to several local charity organizations each year, but I felt like we needed to do more. It struck me that we were living in one of the rainiest locales on the planet but there were people around the world who lived in harsh, dry places where clean drinking water was a precious commodity. I researched several organizations before I chose one whose donations went directly to the projects they were supporting, so I signed up for a fundraising project to build a well. We had to raise at least five thousand dollars to build a well that would provide clean drinking water for a community in need and, once we raised the money, they would tell us where the well would be built. A festival seemed to be the best solution we could think of to raise the money needed to build a well, so I got busy creating plans for Juneau's first and only Water Fest. I assembled a team of our employees and we created fliers, sourced a venue for the event, and we found an incredible local band (Deering & Down), food, and beer donations. Then, we got local tour companies and retail businesses to donate tours and gear for our silent auction. We spent several months planning for the event and it was a huge success! We raised enough money to build the well and later the organization notified us that the well was built in Tigray, Ethiopia. To this day it provides clean drinking water for over four hundred people in that community. There is a plaque with our business name, as well as the city of Juneau,

Alaska on it because we were only able to accomplish that goal with the support of the community.

(Left): Riding a camel in the Sahara. (Right): Matt dressed up as a "Ber-ber".

(Left): Plaque on the well reads: "Alaska Zipline Adventures (The DeSpain Family) & Community of Juneau". (Right) The well we funded in Tigray, Ethiopia.

Do not go where the path may lead, go instead where there is no path and leave a trail. ~Ralph Waldo Emerson

Africa

At the end of that tour season, we finally saved enough money to take a honeymoon trip. We had to delay our plans for a real honeymoon until we could afford it, and we finally reached that point. We had been dreaming of this moment for years. We booked our flight to South Africa and Mauritius and we were on our way. The main reason we chose South Africa was that one of my best friends Sue (my roommate from Tahoe who rubbed ointment on my behind) lived in South Africa with her boyfriend Alex (also one of my roommates in Lake Tahoe), and I was eager to see them and learn more about the country they called home. We landed in Johannesburg, and our friends met us at the airport. I was immediately struck by the dichotomy of wealth so predominantly on display in their beautiful country. On one street we would drive past rows of mud huts and slums while just a couple of minutes down the road you could find high-end shopping centers and restaurants.

We really enjoyed catching up with our friends and hearing about their daily lives in South Africa. A couple of days later, we headed out on a road trip to Kruger National Park. We picked up some provisions along the way, Matt's favorite item by far was the biltong. This was South Africa's version of beef jerky but it tasted infinitely better than anything I had tried in the States. The meat was air dried in large pieces, and instead of cutting the meat into little strips or chunks, they sell it to you whole. You can ask for it "wet" or "dry". We

preferred the wet, or moist, meat and we used a pocket knife
to cut the meat into pieces on the drive.

Sue and Alex thoughtfully planned out this trip for us. We
were able to drive into the park with them, and they arranged
for us to stay in some sweet cabins in the park where animals
roamed freely around us. Each day, we would explore the
park and delight in seeing such stunning creatures in their
natural habitat. Sue is the funniest person I know and she
kept us all laughing with hilarious commentary about the
animals. We ended our days with a sundowner cocktail and a
braai (barbecue). The local meats and fresh vegetables and
fruit were delicious, and we could see why they loved this
place they called home so much.

Sue gave me the book "Cry, the Beloved Country" by Alan
Paton and I read the book each evening in bed while we were
there. When we made our way back to Johannesburg, we
toured the Apartheid Museum and visited a local market. We
wanted to buy something to remember our time in South
Africa with our friends and decided on a pair of fertility
masks. We were hoping to begin trying for a baby after we
returned from the trip and, since I was already thirty-eight
years old, we figured we needed all the help we could get in
that regard. Later that evening we went to a charming
restaurant with an incredible ambiance. The lighting and vibe
were perfect for our last meal with our friends. We enjoyed a
glass of wine and a beautiful meal. Our friends were getting a
little restless towards the end of the meal. They explained to
us that it could be dangerous driving home after dark. They
told us many stories over the years about witnessing crime
and violence in South Africa, but we felt so insulated from all
of that during our visit. We decided it was best to head back
to their place before it got too much later.

The next day, we said our goodbyes and Matt and I rented
a car and drove to Capetown. We marveled at the stunning
vistas from rooftops overlooking the magnificent coastal
city, then we made our way to Table Mountain a couple of
days later. We had decided to go paragliding off Table

Mountain, so we met up with the tour company after hiking around the area. Matt and I were each paired with our tandem partners and, before we knew it, we were running off the side of the mountain and leaping into the air. There was an immediate rush of adrenaline as we left the safety of the ground, but I felt instantly peaceful once we were soaring with the thermals over the city. We flew over the new stadium where the World Cup soccer games were played and we had beautiful views of the ocean and surrounding landscapes.

We landed and shared stories of our experiences, then we watched the sunset over the ocean and drove to a nearby town named Fish Hoek for the night. We woke up the next morning and made our way to a little coffee shop.

I was watching the waves on the beach outside and I said to Matt "This looks like the perfect surf spot for me today. I would love to go out here because the waves are pretty small and consistent and there aren't a lot of rocks."

We inquired about renting surfboards, but they suggested we go out another day when the waves were better, so we went down to Boulder's Beach to see the penguins.

When we returned to the surf shop a few hours later, there was a huge buzz in the shop.

"I still can't believe it. That shark was the size of a dinosaur or even a bus." We overheard the guy working behind the counter say to a customer in disbelief.

I couldn't resist asking "What happened?"

He looked up and said " A Zimbabwean man was here on holiday was swimming about a hundred meters from shore and was attacked by a great white shark. He breached out of the water and appeared to eat him whole."

We were wide-eyed and couldn't say anything in response. We could have easily been swimming in the sea that day and we felt so deeply for the man and his girlfriend who were also there for a relaxing day at the beach.

The following day, we made our way through the Garden Route and on to the Eastern Cape. Then, we made last minute plans to fly to the French Republic of Mauritius. We were arriving at the time of the local Thaipoosum Cavadee Festival, a Hindu festival where devotees proceeded to the local temple in a trance-like state with arrows and limes hanging from piercings on their bodies. It was a sight to see. The bright green limes contrasted with the hot pink silk clothing they wore and their dark skin stood out in front of the pale blue waters of the Indian Ocean behind them. I was mesmerized by it all. I could have stood quietly watching this for days.

On our last day in Mauritius, we decided to book a tour on a small boat to take us out for sunset. We heard about others taking these trips on larger, more expensive boats, but we befriended a local man with a small boat who assured us he could take us to the same spot. We happily hopped on board his boat and, about an hour and a half later, we ran aground, far from shore, because it was low tide. We were marooned in the Indian Sea after sunset. The Captain insisted on entertaining us, while waiting for the tide to come in and lift the boat off the sandbar, by pulling an octopus out of the water and other such things. He was determined to make sure we had a great time. Matt offered to help push the boat off the sandbar but the Captain said it wasn't safe because of the spiny sea urchins below. As kind as that was of him, we had a 6am flight out the next morning and we needed to get back to shore. Thankfully, it seemed the boat was just lodged on a sandbar.

After what felt like hours with no sign of the boat floating off the sandbar, the Captain asked Matt to help pull the boat free.

Matt whispered to me "What about those spiny sea urchins?" as he hopped out and helped the Captain pull the boat off the sandbar.

Eventually we made our way back to shore in the dark. It was a long, quiet ride back to the dock, and it didn't appear that he had a GPS device or depth-finder of any kind. He seemed to be lost and changed directions a couple of times, but we finally made it back to shore and wearily walked to our modest room later that night to pack our belongings for the long flight home.

(Left): Matt, Sue, Rachel, Alex. South Africa. (Right): Lion in Kruger National Park

Me paragliding over Table Mountain in South Africa

(Left): Festival in Mauritius. (Right): Marooned in Mauritius.

Having kids feels like that first seventh-grade crush that overwhelms every molecule in your body, but it's permanent. ~Kristen Bell

Rainbow Baby

The next morning we boarded our eighteen-hour flight from Johannesburg to Atlanta, Georgia where we were thrust back into reality. We were presenting a workshop on zipline tours at a big conference. We prepared our presentation on the plane and hoped the jetlag wouldn't derail us too much. The presentation went smoothly, then we met up with a bunch of our friends from the zipline industry whom we had become good friends with over the years.

We flew back to Bend, Oregon a couple days later where we were able to catch our breath and get over the jetlag. About six weeks after we got back home, I realized that I had missed my period. My "moon", as I call it, was always regular. I was rarely ever late, so when two weeks passed since the time I should have started, I got a pregnancy test. I took the test without much expectation because we had just started trying to have a baby and, at my age, I was aware that it could be years before we could become pregnant, if ever.

I walked out of the bathroom where Matt was sitting on the bed. I think I was partially in shock

"Babe. You won't believe this. I think those fertility masks worked. I'm pregnant!" I couldn't contain my excitement.

"No way!" Matt looked genuinely surprised, and he couldn't hide the giant smile that was spreading across his face.

We embraced and laughed for a while, overflowing with joy, then we began to realize how much this baby was going to change our lives. We were so excited for this next chapter of our lives where we could focus on someone besides ourselves. We were ready to share the joy of this baby with our families and friends but a few weeks later, I woke up with some cramps and bleeding and I called my Mom in the middle of the night. She did a good job of not jumping to any conclusions.

She calmly said "Just get some rest and call your doctor in the morning. There's nothing else you can do right now."

So that's what I did. He got me in for an appointment the same day, and they couldn't find a heartbeat. I had a miscarriage. What struck me when I got home that day is that I couldn't think of a single friend who had a miscarriage. I felt very alone and sad about losing the baby, and I felt like it was my fault somehow. My friends must have known what they were doing more than I did because they were able to have healthy, full-term babies. Obviously, I hadn't read enough, done enough, been enough.

We flew back to Juneau a few weeks later for the start of the tourism season and I threw myself back into work. I never really allowed myself the opportunity to really cry or fully grieve for the baby I had lost. I thought that hiding under a pile of work and staying busy was the best solution.

A few months later, Matt and I made a quick trip back to Oregon for a long weekend and we decided to begin trying again. I missed my next period again, but we knew it would take time to get pregnant again. We bought a couple tests, and we were in total shock when the tests came back positive. This time the excitement was even greater because we fully appreciated what a fragile opportunity this was with my age and a miscarriage already behind us. We cried tears of joy together in silence. Words wouldn't have been able to capture our feelings in that moment. We never fully realized how ready we were to be parents until that experience was taken away from us the first time, and we weren't taking any of this for granted this time around.

We waited until I was 12 weeks pregnant to tell our family and friends. I was cautiously optimistic and thought I was handling things pretty well. Then, our friends Emily and Bryan were staying with us, and she asked if she could see the baby's room. We walked in together and I opened the drawers to show her some of the baby's clothes.

She said "Oh Rach, I think it's okay to take the tags off now".

I hadn't realized that I was leaving an escape route in case things didn't work out again this time. I took the tags off the baby clothes the next morning. It felt so good to finally feel like the baby was safe and that our dream was becoming a reality.

My friends in Alaska threw a phenomenal baby shower for me. They made a beautiful cake, delicious food, and created the perfect, relaxed atmosphere. I didn't like to be the center of attention, but there was no denying that this was a special moment. My girl-friends contacted my husband before the shower to ask him some questions. Then, they asked me the same questions and we all laughed when comparing our answers.

The main question that stood out was "What feature of Rachel's do you hope the baby gets?" I said "my nose" because he always said I had a cute nose. His answer blew me away. He said "her feistiness". *Oh shit. Really? Does he actually want more of that?* I wondered.

We had a great evening talking about the baby, enjoying my favorite pregnancy food-soup and panini sandwiches-and opening presents with my friends. There was so much joy swirling around the room that night, and I was overflowing with gratitude.

We flew back to Bend, Oregon for the winter and the months flew by. I was really enjoying the more relaxed lifestyle we were living. The morning of my first ultrasound, we went for a strenuous hike and the baby was barely moving. The doctor was a little concerned but he said that hopefully she was just tired from the hike just like her

Mommy. We were having a girl! I was hoping for a curly haired tom-girl and I was so excited. I built the furniture for our baby's room and I painted a picture for her wall. Matt packed our bags for the hospital about two months early, so every time I went somewhere, he would check in wondering if this was the time.

A couple of days before the baby was due, we decided to take our snow machine up the mountain to play. Normally, Matt and I would take turns driving the snow machine and towing behind on our skis or snowboard. That day, I had to stick to driving the snow machine while Matt snowboarded because I thought it would be too risky to ski, but we had a great time playing in the snow that day.

One day after my due date, I made an appointment to be seen by my doctor because something didn't feel right. My doctor was out of town, so I met another doctor at the hospital that day. He did an ultrasound and he said there was no longer any fluid in the placenta and we needed to get the baby out. He said "Meet me at the hospital. You are going to have a baby". I called my husband and told him to meet me there; he was shocked.

We talked to Grandpa Deez the night before and he told us that he was going to enter a snowmachine contest called the "Tired Iron". It was designed for people ninety years of age or older.

He said "I'm going to try to win the race for your daughter." This is the write up they posted for the race "Remember, this is about having fun and showing off some cool, old iron. We hold the right to change the rules as we go along. Any air or liquid-cooled sled up to, and including, 1979 model year may compete. Race to be held at Jurassic Park. We'll kick off with the Battle of the Ageless for participants 90 & up for drivers that still have their faculties, but not necessarily their original teeth, hips, or knees."

We met the doctor at the hospital on a snowy day, and he induced labor with Pitocin. After ten hours of hard posterior labor, the pain was increasing exponentially and the baby's heart rate was dropping close to zero. Finally, the doctor looked at me and said "I'm sorry Rachel. The baby has gone into a breech position and we need to move to an emergency C-Section." I looked at him and said "What are you waiting for? Let's do this." About thirty minutes later, we welcomed our sweet baby girl Zoelle into this world. We got a call shortly afterwards that Grandpa Deez won the Tired Iron, Battle of the Ageless race for our daughter. Apparently, at ninety years of age and driving a 1969 Caribou snowmachine, he got lost during the race, but he still managed to win.

As much as our new baby filled my heart with joy the moment she was born, I think what I treasured most was sharing our joy with our families and friends. There was a sea of love floating around and it was an incredible feeling to take it all in. For example, handing our baby to our Moms and watching them take her in with such wonder and amazement was a moment I will never forget. Seeing everyone hold her and play with her and develop their own relationships with her was such a heart-warming experience. She was our rainbow baby, and I loved sharing her with our village.

On a deeper level, our daughter filled every empty space in my heart so that I no longer felt any voids. She healed places inside of me that I had no idea were broken. We were overflowing with joy. And exhaustion.

Me, Matt, Zoe & Zihua.

The journey is learning that pain, like love, is simply something to surrender to. It's a holy space we can enter with people only if we promise not to tidy up. ~Glennon Doyle

Bull of the Woods

Matt and I found a class being offered through the local community college that taught students how to build their own wooden stand-up paddleboard. We immediately signed up and decided that these weekly classes would be our opportunity to do something for ourselves during a time that was otherwise focused on parenting. The class was held once a week in the evening, so we found an incredible babysitter who came over to keep an eye on Zoe while we learned how to build wooden boards. This became a big hobby of ours, and we built several boards of different shapes and sizes in our workshop. These boards deepened our love for wood-working, especially for Matt who has continued to build some beautiful furniture and custom decks, among other things.

That year, when we returned to Alaska for the tourism season, I enjoyed the challenge of juggling our new baby and the business we had grown from scratch. I nursed her during our company meetings, and our staff enjoyed playing with her. I loved the feeling that we were one big, extended family. We really cared about our team, and they cared about us too.

For several years in a row, we went to the tiny, coastal town of Haines on the ferry for the Southeast Alaska State Fair. When I first met Matt, I thought he was shy and I couldn't have imagined him doing anything to draw attention to himself. So, he surprised me when he decided to enter the logging/lumberjack competition at the fair for the first time. Some of the events, like axe throwing, were fairly tame, but others like the choker-setting competition required the competitors to run over the tops of huge logs with heavy steel cable in their arms. The other guys were practicing running up and over the logs that were lying on the ground, and Matt entered the competition without an opportunity to practice. He thought he could just jump across the logs from the top without having to go up and down the sides of each one like everyone else. He was 6'5" tall, but I thought it was pretty risky for him to try it during the actual competition without practicing it beforehand. There were lots of spectators in the stands, and we all watched together in suspense as Matt glided from the top of one tree to the next with ease and totally smoked the competition.

He asked me last-minute if I would enter the Jack & Jill Hand-bucking event with him. He knew how much I hated public performances of any kind, so I knew he really wanted me to do it.

"Okay, fine. I will do it for you, but only because I love you so much".

I had a tie dye skirt on with flip flops. That wasn't exactly the traditional attire for a Lumber Jill. But we asked the MC of the event to watch Zoe for us, and I went out there and did it for my man. I loved him immensely and always wanted to support his passions. It was so fun to watch him compete in those events. He really rose to the occasion, and I was in awe of how he could beat some of the younger guys out there. He entered several events and he won the most points overall of all the men that entered, so he was named the "Bull of the Woods." He went on to win that title two more times. One year, Matt decided to enter the Gold Rush Days logging competition in Juneau. The people who entered the competition in Juneau typically had more experience, so Matt entered just for fun. He convinced our good friend Nolan, an Alaskan bush pilot and dentist, to join him for the choker-setting event. They had so much fun. It was so sweet to share those moments with our friends. What a unique life we were living!

That year, for my fortieth birthday, Matt collaborated with some of my girlfriends to throw a big party. They decided on a Texas-themed party at the Ski Area Lodge where our zipline tour offices and shop were located. Matt rented a big barbecue pit and he built a big axe target for axe-throwing. The girls put together some really fun decorations including a hilarious sheet cake with a photo of me from high school on it that they somehow managed to get from my Mom. We had such a fun time and the axe-throwing was such a big hit that we added it to our zipline tour. When our guests finished the tour, they capped their experience off with some good old fashioned axe throwing. We were proud to offer that experience to our guests way before axe-throwing became a popular activity in urban bars across the country.

At the end of the tourism season, we always threw an epic party for our crew. They worked so hard all summer, so we felt that was the least we could do to thank them. That year, we organized a trade with one of the local helicopter companies. In exchange for taking all of their staff out of our tour, we were able to take all of our guides out on a helicopter tour over the beautiful waterfalls and glaciers in the area. The year before, we had taken our team out on a helicopter and landed on a glacier where we all went dog-sledding on the glacier. That year, we decided to take them all to the thrift shop to buy some funky clothes for the occasion, then we blindfolded them and arrived at the helicopter pad where we took off for sightseeing. We had them remove their blindfolds, and they screamed and jumped up and down with excitement. We went on a helicopter ride over the glacier ice fields, and we had the best time despite the rainy weather. Afterwards, we landed at a lodge and stayed overnight. Some of the other celebrations we organized involved kayaking to a glacier and whale watching with a stop on an island for a cookout. We would share laughs, give the team thank you gifts and sometimes the crew would come up with awards to give each other. Our staff felt like family to us and they often gave us cards and gifts that brought us to tears.

After the tourism season wrapped up in Alaska, we flew to San Diego where I met up with Tara to do the 3-Day Breast Cancer Walk with her. When I met Matt, I had volunteered to help set up and break-down the event, this time I wanted to actually walk the event (twenty miles per day over the course of three days). We had a great time walking over hills along the coast together even though I got several blisters and lost a couple of toenails from the long days of walking. I was still nursing Zoe, so Matt would bring her to meet up with us on lunch breaks and I would nurse her while I grabbed a bite to eat. It felt great to raise money for a cause I cared about and revisit the event where I met Matt all those years ago.

We spent the next few years going back and forth between Alaska and Oregon. We would stay in Alaska from March until October for the tourism season and we would soak up the quiet, snowy winters in Bend, Oregon with our daughter. We delighted in watching her experience the world. Each time she saw a new animal she would squeal with excitement. Then, she took her first steps and said her first words. We were fully enthralled with each moment and our parents were equally enraptured.

Mom flew to Oregon during the Fall to visit us and see her friend in Portland. She had quit her job, so she had time to enjoy sightseeing with us while the leaves changed into impossible shades of neon orange, yellow and red. We took her to a pumpkin patch where she was able to enjoy playing with her Granddaughter. We drove her to Crater Lake and she even made some snowballs with the remaining snow left on the tops of the mountains. That was a very special and memorable trip but I noticed something different about Mom. She had lost some weight and she didn't seem like herself. I tried to check in with her gently because Mom always made it clear that she called the shots and she didn't want anyone meddling in her business. She was adamant that everything was fine and under control and that was the end of the subject.

Over the next couple years Mom's health continued to deteriorate but she wouldn't really share the details of what was going on. She finally told us that she had Mastocytosis (a rare condition caused by an excess number of mast cells gathering in the body's tissues), and the doctors told her she only had a couple of years left to live. Apparently, when someone has this condition from a young age, it can develop into a more serious problem later in life if it's left untreated.

After I hung up the phone with Mom from that conversation, I felt numb. I was in shock and disbelief, but eventually reality began to sink in. Not long after her diagnosis, Mom began having suicidal feelings. I think she was feeling helpless and exhausted from all of the health issues she was having. She would post on Facebook that she was ending her life, then I would call to check on her and she wouldn't answer her phone. If I couldn't reach her or John within a few minutes, I would leave a message letting her know I was going to call the police department near her house and have them check on her. So, after not hearing back from her or John, I called the police department and explained what happened and asked if they would check on her. They drove over and let me know how things were going.

At first, she answered the door and apologized, and they left. That happened several times, then one day Mom left a message for me and John, while we were both at work, that she had a knife and was going to kill herself. When I couldn't reach her, I began to panic and called the police and told them what she said. I was terrified that my biggest fear had come true, that Mom had taken her own life. When the police knocked on her door that day and she eventually let them in, they explained that they had to take her to the hospital because she told all of us that she had a knife and was planning to kill herself. They put Mom on a 51/50 hold, and they brought her to a mental health facility where she was required to stay for a few days. Mom was upset about being taken there initially, but she eventually slept really well and enjoyed getting to know some of the other patients. She was required to attend counseling sessions while she was there, and when she returned home I was hopeful that she would continue with therapy. I had tried many times over the years to talk to Mom about seeing a therapist, to no avail. I was devastated when she told me, once again, that she didn't have any interest in therapy and the matter was no longer up for discussion. I knew that what she was going through must have been so difficult for her, and it pained me to see her shouldering those challenges on her own. I recognized my own needs for help during that time, and I found a great therapist who was enormously beneficial in assisting me to process my feelings of anxiety and frustration while maintaining my love and support for my mom. I was determined to stay the course with my mom because I loved her so dearly, and my therapist helped me realize the critical importance of setting healthy boundaries that allowed me to be there for Mom while also making sure my needs and those of husband and daughter weren't being neglected.

I wasn't sleeping very well during that time because I stayed awake worrying about Mom each night. So, Matt selflessly decided to give me some time to take a nap one day. He took Zoe to the store to pick up some groceries, and he took our dog Z along so she could go for a walk. When he returned home with the groceries, he had Zoe in the car seat in one hand, and an armful of groceries in the other hand. He called Z out of the car the same way we had each time we got home. She always jumped out and stayed right by our sides, following us back down the stairs to our condo. This time, something caught her attention on the other side of the road, and Z bolted to chase after it. Unfortunately, a car hit her before she reached the other side. Matt picked Z up off the road, and she was still breathing. He called me and told me what happened and told me he was taking Z to the vet.

"Oh no! I want to come with you!" I begged.

"I'm already on the way there. I need you to call the vet and tell him I'm coming." He said with urgency and pain emanating through his words.

So, I did. Unfortunately, Z stopped breathing in Matt's arms on the way to the vet. I didn't even have a chance to tell her goodbye. We were absolutely devastated by the loss of our sweet pup. We cried for a few months after she passed, and it felt like the pain would never end.

Life had been really good for a while, and we had a great run, but nothing good lasts forever. We realized that we were juggling different priorities and being pulled in new directions with a young child at home and Mom's health declining while trying to keep our zipline business afloat. Ultimately, we made the decision to sell our zipline tour to a sweet couple who managed the business for us for the past few years. A year later we moved to the lower 48 where we planned to soak up the joys of parenthood. We wanted to be midway between our families so we could go back to see my family a little easier and still be able to get back to Alaska to see Matt's family as well. We bought an old fixer-upper house on some land with a pond and a big shop on Bainbridge Island, across from Seattle in Washington.

(Left: Me, Mom & Zoe). (Right): Matt and Zoe having fun at the glacier, Juneau, AK.

(Left): Matt and I, Mendenhall glacier. (Right): Matt throwing axes at the fair.

(Left): Matt & I competing in the Jack & Jill hand-bucking competition.

Words are like nets. We hope they'll cover what we mean, but we know they can't possibly hold that much joy, or grief, or wonder. ~Jodi Picoult

Squirrel Coffee

O ver the next few years, we remodeled the house and built wooden stand-up paddleboards in the shop. We enjoyed our peaceful lives there. We often rode our bikes to the ferry, then biked into Seattle when the ferry arrived on the other side. We explored the city on our bikes and marveled over the beauty of summer days in Seattle. We had an old used boat that we took over to the San Juan Islands during the summer, and Zoe loved to watch the orcas as we would fish for crab and halibut.

We made a great group of friends there. They had a diverse range of careers from doctor to hovercraft pilot. One of our friends named Skip, a former musician, was renovating an old dilapidated farmhouse into a stunning home that is worthy of being in a magazine. His wife had a high level consulting job in Seattle, and she commuted into the city on the ferry each day. It was always entertaining to hang out with them and hear about their latest adventures. One day, they told us about how they were fed up with tending to the yard and their lawnmower died, so they bought some goats and brought them home in the minivan. As they were driving home with their kids, they smelled something awful, so they looked in the back and realized the goats had relieved themselves in the van. Another time we were visiting with them, Skip explained that he decided to make his own beekeeper suit and he made it out of wool. When he was tending to the bees, they swarmed around him and got into his suit and he was stung countless times that day. We were so enthralled by their homesteading lifestyle that we would lie awake in bed discussing our own dreams of building a life like that for our family.

One day on a walk near our house, I discovered a woodpecker that appeared to be injured. He was standing in the middle of the trail and didn't seem to move as I approached him. I bent down to get a closer look at him, and I really began to worry about his condition. I called a wildlife shelter and they agreed with my assessment. They instructed me to try to put the bird in a box with holes for ventilation and bring him right in. I went home, got a box, and told Matt and Zoe. They decided to join me on the journey to the shelter. We hopped in the car with hope and optimism, feeling proud of ourselves for saving this beautiful creature. We walked into the shelter and the in-take person asked me to fill out a form, then she asked if I'd like her to let me know how the bird was doing.

I immediately said "Yes".

Then she replied back quickly "He didn't make it".

I erupted into tears, not the quiet kind either. I was not prepared for her to tell me right then and there and I certainly wasn't prepared for that outcome.

We came here to save a bird, dammit. My child is with me, can't you see? Oh, wait a minute. I'm the one who is a crying mess here. Pull yourself together.

Matt thought the whole thing was adorable and sweet that I cared so much to sob over a bird I just met. I didn't think it was sweet or cute at all. I cried all the way home.

Matt left for a hunting trip with Gil shortly after that, so Tara came to visit so we could enjoy some girl time. My only concern while he was gone was that Matt had been putting out traps for the wild family of raccoons that was digging up our property and eating the neighbors' chickens every night. He trapped the raccoons, then drove them across the bridge into Kingston where he released them. I asked him to please be sure none of the traps were set while he was away because I wasn't comfortable dealing with angry caged up raccoons.

On the first night of Tara's visit, we heard a shrieking noise. So, the next morning when it was light outside, we walked around to see if anything was wrong. We walked into the woods and sure enough the first thing we saw was a pair of beady eyes peering up at us from inside a cage.

"Dammit" I said. "Matt promised me he would dismantle the traps".

"Shit, what do we do now?" Tara asked.

"I think we have to put the raccoon in the back of Matt's truck and release it".

So we put a long stick through the cage and each grabbed one side of it and carried the raccoon together to the truck. We put the cage in the back of the truck and drove over the bridge to Kingston. When we got there, we found a nice spot, turned off the truck and walked around to the tailgate. When we peeked over the bed of the truck, the raccoon made the loudest, angriest shriek and jumped at us. Yes, he was still in the cage, but he was not happy and we were nervous about releasing him. We tried to unhook the latch, but it wasn't working properly, so we couldn't get it open. About that time, a police officer pulled up and asked us what we were doing.

We just told him the truth, straight up. "We are trying to release this delinquent raccoon into the wild, but the cage isn't cooperating. Can you help us?"

So, the officer peeked over the bed of the truck, and the raccoon pulled the same jump and hiss-shriek maneuver, and the officer jumped backwards

"Damn! That thing scared me." He apologized for not being more helpful and got back in his car.

I started the truck, and Tara and I used a stick to finally pry open the cage, then ran like hell to the front of the truck and hopped in and closed the doors. By the time we reached the front of the truck, the raccoon was already standing on the side of the truck bed, looking angry, and lunging towards us. He was not playing around. He quickly jumped down and headed into the woods, and we made our way home. On our drive back, I saw a squirrel run in front of the truck and tried to stop but I was too late. I squealed and pulled over. I got out of the truck, and saw that the squirrel was dead. I burst into tears and found some leaves and covered the squirrel and moved him to the side of the road. Poor sweet squirrel. I hope she had a good life. I hope her mother could find it in her heart to forgive me. Tara and I got back into the truck, but I was an inconsolable mess. I couldn't stop crying for the longest time. I wasn't prepared to drive for a while, so finally we decided that we should just go get a cup of coffee and regroup. It had been quite a morning. We pulled into the coffee shop, ordered our coffee and sat down. The barista brought our coffees over to us and she put Tara's cup down with a beautiful leaf painted into the foam. When the barista put my cup down in front of me, I thought I was hallucinating.

"Stop it! Tara, please tell me that is not what I think it is!" I slowly pushed my coffee cup over to Tara, my eyes still swollen from the incident that just happened. She looked inside my cup

"No way! That's crazy, Rach!" The barista had made squirrel art in my coffee! Nobody had ever made squirrel art in my coffee before this day. *Why now?* I was somehow laughing and crying at the same time as I took a photo of it, then pathetically drank my coffee until the squirrel-foam disappeared.

Tara and I left for a backpacking trip to Whistler Mountain in Canada the next day. We camped and marveled over the stunning alpine scenery. It was a fantastic trip, although we set off in the snow but it never accumulated too much.

I made some great girlfriends on Bainbrdge Island, and we had some stellar "girls' nights" together. We enjoyed delicious meals and great conversation, and the evenings would usually end with late night dancing and lots of laughter. We were building a great life there, but we were growing tired of the rain. The summers were glorious in the

Pacific Northwest, but we'd spent a lot of years in the rain just waiting for those precious months when the sun would finally peek out. We wanted to move to a place where we could play outside year-round more easily.

A consulting opportunity arose in Florida and we decided to take it. We never quite imagined living there, but we decided that a gap year in Florida was just what the doctor ordered. Mom was getting sicker and depression was sinking into my bones. The sunshine and turquoise waters were so healing for all of us. I was able to make the drive back to see Mom several times and Zoe was so enamored by the warm waters and beach time that she didn't notice how sad I was. The beach also provided Matt with some reprieve on the days that he had to watch over Zoe while I was on the phone for hours trying to help coordinate hospice care for Mom.

One night when I was talking to Mom, I asked her if she had enough strength for a weekend in New Orleans. It was one of her favorite places, and I wondered if we could meet in the middle there. The long drives to Florida and back were hard to pull off with a young child at home and work, but it struck me that this could be a welcome change of pace for Mom, too.

"Yes! That sounds great, Baby." she said without hesitation.

So, we packed our bags and the three of us jumped in the car and made our way to New Orleans. Mom and John met us there where we had oysters together and listened to jazz musicians playing in the streets. Those were two of Mom's favorite things but I could see that she was wasting away. She had lost so much weight that she looked like skin and bones and she bruised so easily. She was not happy anymore, so those fleeting moments of seeing her in a place that she loved and not imprisoned in her own home were precious.

(Left) Squirrel coffee. (Middle) Matt building a paddleboard. (Right) Finished board.

(Left) Zoe & me, Bend, OR. (Right) Zoe, Bainbridge Island, WA.

Tara & I backpacking, Whistler Mountain

There are no goodbyes for us. Wherever you are, you will always be in my heart.
~Gandhi

North Star

After Mom returned home to Austin, her health continued to decline. We drove back to spend Thanksgiving with her and she couldn't get up from her chair at all. Mom's greatest joy was cooking, and that was the first time in my life that we had Thanksgiving without Mom in the kitchen. It didn't feel the same. I just wanted to skip over Thanksgiving because there wasn't much to be thankful for, and it just seemed to highlight how different everything was from years past.

It was all happening so fast. Mom got sicker by the minute, and it was like she was aging at warp speed. She didn't want to go outside anymore, so she spent each day sitting in the recliner in her living room with all the shades drawn so no natural light could come in. Somehow her sickness managed to suck the life and happiness right out of her. She didn't have the desire to keep living; she was ready to be at peace and out of pain. I wrote her letters and cards, decorated her house, and tried to make sure she knew just how much I loved her and how much she would be missed. I know she understood, but it didn't make things any easier.

The realization really sunk in on that visit that Mom wouldn't make it much longer. I sat with her on her chair and played a video I took for her of Zoe singing in a school performance, and she asked me to play it over and over again. Zoe crawled up into her lap and just sat with her for hours. For our active five year old child, sitting in one place like that for so long was a first. She is a sensitive girl who picks up on things very quickly, so I think she knew how

much her Grandma "Nini" needed those cuddles at that
moment. It was difficult to leave to go back to Florida after
that visit. I wasn't sure how much longer Mom would live,
and I couldn't bear the thought of not being there by her
side.

We booked a flight to go back to Austin for Christmas so
we could be together for the holidays and I talked to Mom
and the nurses from the hospice every day. I was desperate
to find out how she was doing so I could tell if she was
declining, but Mom and the nurses gave me the same
answers each day. I asked John to let me know if she took a
turn for the worse, but I would lie awake in bed each night
worrying that she might die in her sleep. I woke up one
morning with severe chest pains and I went to the doctor to
make sure everything was okay. He said I was experiencing
severe anxiety and tried to prescribe me some strong anti-
anxiety medication. I refused to take the medicine because I
needed to be mentally strong enough to keep tabs on Mom
and talk to her nurses.

I called my cousin Leigh, who is an incredibly smart doctor,
one day and asked for her advice on how to determine if
Mom was getting worse. She was so compassionate and
helpful and said one of the things we should look for is fluid
building up in her abdomen. One morning shortly after that,
I was talking to John and asking about Mom and I asked
about fluid in her abdomen.

He said "Oh yeah, I noticed that her stomach has swelled
up quite a bit". A long silence sat between us.

I finally managed to say "Oh no. I need to figure out how
to get there sooner".

The flights we were booked on didn't depart for another
week, so Pam helped us arrange for new flights that arrived
in two days, and we cancelled our other tickets. We checked
into the airport, and they told us the flight was delayed
several hours. I couldn't speak. All I could think about was
how each hour we would spend in the airport was time we

wouldn't have with Mom. I felt like I was going to lose my mind, so I took Zoe for a walk in the airport and we went into one of the shops and bought the biggest bag of Hershey's Kisses I could find. I was determined to find some joy in those moments. We boarded the plane, and I asked Zoe if she wanted to pass out Hershey's Kisses to everyone on the plane who had been waiting so long for the delayed flight. She was thrilled with the idea. So, our sweet 5 year old girl who loved her Nini walked down each row of the plane handing out chocolates to distressed passengers, and we listened and watched while people smiled, laughed, and thanked her. We all enjoyed a few moments of joy from that simple act.

We landed in Austin and I felt somber. I knew what laid ahead of us, and it wasn't going to be easy. I wasn't ready to say goodbye to my Mom. She was a strong woman who didn't like to talk about difficult circumstances like this, so I had struggled to find the right words to address the fact that she was dying. I wrote her countless letters telling her how deeply I loved her, what a great Mother she was and how I would always keep her memory alive, but I couldn't summon the courage to say all of those things to her face.

When we got to the house, she was lying in bed in the office. Her face was gaunt, and I could barely see any trace of the Mother I had known and loved since the day I was born.

I walked out of the room for a minute to gain my composure and fearfully said to Matt, "This is happening".

Then I returned to the office with Mom and sat by her side and held her hand. I played her favorite songs for her, and I kept repeating "I love you" to her, like a broken record. I couldn't seem to string together any other words during that time. I was afraid if I tried to say anything else, I would fall apart, and I wanted to stay strong for Mom so she could be at peace. For the first time in my life, I was at a loss for words.

We were so torn about how to convey all of this to Zoe. I had unknowingly become a Bulldozer Parent. These are the people who try to remove any obstacles in their child's way. I was just in the process of realizing what I had become and trying to figure out how it all happened. Ultimately, I realized that I had feelings of not being safe as a child. Even though I knew how much Mom loved me, I didn't always feel safe and protected. Those stifled feelings from my childhood somehow resurfaced and manifested themselves as being an overprotective parent. Also, I think my independent nature stemmed from not feeling protected as a child. I quickly learned how to take care of things myself and adopted the belief that I couldn't rely on others to keep me safe. But, now I had become the parent who went to the pet store late one night to buy an identical replacement fish for the one that died so my daughter wouldn't notice the next morning. I truly thought that I was helping her and saving her from pain. I was doing anything and everything in my power to prevent her from experiencing any challenge or struggle. One day a good friend of mine sat down and explained to me that when we prevent our children from experiencing sadness, grief and pain, we are also preventing them from learning how to deal with those feelings and emotions. She further explained that what our children really need is to experience pain and disappointment so they can be better prepared for life's inevitable curveballs.

If I prevented her from experiencing all of this pain in her childhood, what would she do when she became an adult and faced loss and heart-break?

I was mortified to realize my best intentions for loving and protecting my child were actually stifling her and doing her harm. This eye-opening moment happened just as Mom was dying. I was grateful to have realized this while Mom was still alive. I wrote her a letter to thank her for instilling grit and determination in me from such a young age. If she had coddled me and protected me from pain, I wouldn't be the person I am today who is capable of handling struggle. Still, I was consumed with the dilemma of what to tell Zoe about my mom's inevitable death. I decided to tell her the truth: Nini was sick and she was going to die, but I stopped short of allowing her to see it happen. So, we rented a room nearby and Matt and Zoe stayed there for a few nights. They were able to see Mom and give her a hug, but they left shortly thereafter because we just thought it would be too hard for a five year old child to process.

As I sat beside Mom and held her hand in silence, the gravity of the situation was so much bigger than I could grasp. Mom was going to die. The time was coming, and I could feel the moment growing closer. Every breath she took was more labored and she was sleeping most of the time. I wanted so badly to find the words to say that would take her pain away or make her better, but I couldn't. I just told her that I loved her, played her favorite songs for her, and I fully absorbed every laugh or smile she was able to muster.

After an excruciating few days of struggle, I woke up early one morning and asked Matt if he could come stay the night with me, Mom and John. I had a feeling that this might be Mom's last day, so Pam kept Zoe that night at her house. I'm so glad he was there by my side that night because Mom had a really rough night and he was so helpful and supportive to me and John. She was struggling a lot and it was so incredibly hard to see her go through all of that.

She hadn't spoken or opened her eyes for the past couple days, but Matt leaned over to her and whispered "I promise to always take care of your girls." Mom immediately sat up, opened her eyes, and gave Matt a kiss on the cheek. I'm not sure where she summoned the awareness and strength to do that, but it was a very powerful moment. I was so comforted to know that Mom was hearing and processing all of the loving things we were saying and doing in her final days.

At one point later that night when we were taking turns resting, I leaned over to Mom and held her hand and said "You were such a great Mom, and I'll always love you."

I knew the moment was coming for a while, but somehow nothing quite prepares you for it. Mom took her last breath before dawn, on the morning of the winter solstice. I had a big, long, hard cry. I felt like I had failed her somehow. This time I couldn't save her. I was afraid of what life would be like without her. She was still the one I would call when I had a hard day and she was also the first person I talked to when something good was happening in my life. She was my confidant, my North Star. I felt as though my compass had broken, and I wouldn't be able to find my way without her.

Peace comes from within. Do not seek it without. ~Gautama Buddha

Lost at Sea

After Mom died, I felt numb for a while. I noticed the sun was continuing to rise and set, and I was amazed that the world continued on despite the weight of my sadness. We took Zoe out to the beach everyday to get fresh air. I was able to get out of bed and get through the days somehow, but I just felt empty. Hollow. I felt as though I needed to fill myself back up with love and purpose that had drained out of me. There was a hole in my heart that I had no clue how to repair.

I threw a Celebration of Life for Mom. She didn't want a traditional funeral and burial, so we had her cremated and we invited a small handful of family and friends who knew Mom best. We had a potluck lunch at an adorable winery that Mom would have loved. We shared stories and memories of Mom and did our best to stay positive that day. She didn't want people crying in fancy black clothes, so we celebrated her life together casually with food and wine.

I held it together for a while, but when the time came for me to say a few words, I got to the part about how much she loved her grand-daughter and I choked up. I felt as though my airways ceased and I couldn't breathe. I wanted to be strong for Zoe, so I took a couple deep breaths, and continued. Once I finished my speech, I was able to relax and take in the love that was emanating from the people who loved mom the most. It was comforting to be able to celebrate her precious life and all the good that she brought into this world.

While we were in Austin for Mom's celebration, we decided to move back home. My Stepdad John lost his Mom only three days before Mom passed away, and he didn't really have any other family checking in on him at the time. I felt like we needed to go home for a while. We had lived in Alaska, closer to Matt's family, for almost a decade, and we finally had the freedom work-wise to move back to Austin to be closer to my family for a while.

So, we packed up our things and we were on the road again. We quickly settled in the hills around Lake Travis. This is one of my favorite parts of Austin, and we spent as much time as we could hiking, biking and boating around the lake. Quickly, we had to get work going again so we started a business building outdoor spaces- pergolas, patios, outdoor kitchens, and fire pits. Matt had years of experience with carpentry and construction, so it was a great fit. I handled the website and communications side of things, and he was the General Contractor overseeing these projects. Work took off quickly and we realized the location was perfect because there were so many new homes being built in the area.

My friend Jenny from high school has selflessly fostered dozens of animals over the years, and I noticed on Facebook that she was fostering a sweet lab mix named Mariposa, Spanish for "butterfly". She had been rescued from a shelter in a run-down Mexican border town and Jenny was providing a perfect landing place for her until she found her forever home. Mariposa's ribs were showing and she had several infections. She had to be treated at the vet for some of these issues and get spayed.

Jenny said if nobody else adopted her, she would take her because Mariposa was such a sweet girl. The timing was right for our family. It had been several years since Z passed away, and we finally felt ready to get another dog. Zoe was six and would enjoy having a pet and could learn about the responsibilities involved with taking care of an animal. I showed the picture to Matt and we both knew that she was our pup. We filled out the application and when we found out it was going to be approved, we told Zoe and she was over the moon! This would be the sister we couldn't give her in real life, a best furry friend.

We picked up Mariposa and brought her home. She was about one year old and she had never walked up stairs. So, we put treats on each stair and we encouraged her to get up and down. She was an absolute dream from the moment we got her, and she completed our family in ways we never imagined.

Around that time, I heard about an upcoming Chili Cook-off. These competitions are a big deal in Texas. People take their chili very seriously. I thought it would be nice to pay homage to Mom because she loved to cook and she made the best chili. Matt and I made several batches of chili the week before the cook-off so we could perfect our recipe. We smoked the brisket meat for a long time, and we dialed-in all the spices.

The day of the cook-off was a cold January morning. Lots of our friends and family showed up that day for the event. We had a great time visiting with everyone and we honestly thought we didn't have a shot at the contest because we had never entered a cooking competition of any kind. We got lucky and somehow managed to win first place in the Cook-off. I know Mom was watching over us that day and loved every moment of that experience. That win was definitely for her, and she was with us in spirit.

We were making lots of friends in the neighborhood, and Zoe was enjoying her new school. For the first two years, things were going pretty well for all of us. We had saved up for a trip to the Virgin Islands over Spring Break, and it finally felt like we were getting our lives on track. That was the trip when I felt the shooting pain in my breast. After we came back from that trip, everything was a blur.

After my diagnosis, Matt and I decided to keep the babysitter we had scheduled for that night. Our good friend Christie was in town and we were planning to go to an event her company was putting on in downtown Austin. We weren't ready to tell Zoe about my diagnosis, so the two of us went out for dinner and strategized about how we wanted to proceed and how we planned to tell her. There was a lot of love between us that night. Our spirits were surprisingly good and we felt optimistic and strong. We sat outside on a cliff overlooking the lake and laughed together, clearly not processing the scope of what was ahead of us. While we were talking that night, my Oncologist called. I was shocked to get a call from her after 6pm before we had even met in person. She told me that she was going to squeeze me in for an appointment as she was aware that waiting was often the hardest part.

I met with my Oncologist the following day, and she explained that I could either have a lumpectomy with radiation or a mastectomy. She said that most women in my position opt for a lumpectomy with radiation because a mastectomy is a more serious surgery and they remove the entire breast. My HER2 results came in as negative, so I was officially diagnosed with IDC ER+, PR+, HER2-. This meant my breast cancer was estrogen fed.

My immediate feelings were that I wanted to have the mastectomy. I was forty-seven years old, and it wasn't as though I had the breasts of a twenty-year old anymore. I had the love of my family and my health, and my life felt more important to me than keeping my breasts. In lieu of opting for a single mastectomy, I chose to pursue a more aggressive approach with a double mastectomy. My thoughts were that I wanted to have all my breast tissue removed to minimize the risk of the cancer spreading or coming back. I was also hoping to avoid radiation. So, they scheduled me for a double mastectomy with immediate breast reconstruction.

This particular surgery can take up to fourteen hours because they remove tissue from the stomach and use microsurgery techniques to reattach the blood vessels from the tissue to the breast area, so I was aware this would be a huge procedure. They scheduled me for a breast MRI. They gave me a contrast solution and they put me face-down on a metal table that moved inside the MRI tunnel. The man who performed the procedure gave me a button to hold and explained that I could press the button if I couldn't go on, but he made sure I was aware that we would have to start over again if that happened. There was a spot around my collar bone that was pressing on the metal table, and after being in the machine for quite a while, I almost had to hit the button. My collar bone was in excruciating pain, and I felt like I was going to throw up from the contrast. I barely made it through and when I came out of the machine, I said "That was awful."

I went home that afternoon, and I put myself into bed and cried hard for a couple hours. Everything was sinking in and I was physically and mentally exhausted from the strain of it all. I didn't get out of bed again for the rest of the day. The results of the MRI were able to show the tumor in my left breast that the mammogram was unable to decipher through my dense breast tissue. The imaging also showed a suspicious spot in my right breast, and my Oncologist wanted to have a biopsy taken of the tissue to confirm whether it was cancerous, but I asked her what the point would be of doing the biopsy if they were going to be removing both of my breasts in the upcoming double mastectomy anyway? She agreed and said she was reassured that the MRI did not show any lymph node involvement.

The following week, I was scheduled for a CT scan of my abdomen because they would be removing tissue from my stomach to create my new breasts and they needed to have a "roadmap" for the surgery. There would be microsurgery required to connect the blood vessels from my stomach tissue to the blood vessels in my breast area. After the surgery, they would keep me in a warm blanket and place a doppler ultrasound on my breast to listen to the blood flow to confirm that the new tissue was accepted and blood was flowing properly.

When I went in for the CT scan, I was still a little wary after the uncomfortable MRI experience, but the technician explained this would be a very different experience. She injected the contrast solution into my veins and she told me the most uncomfortable part of this exam would be that I was going to feel like I was peeing during the scan although she assured me that wouldn't really happen. I was able to lie on my back for the procedure and the table moved into a tunnel-like machine similar to the one they used for the MRI. The CT scan was more tolerable for me than the MRI.

I was getting so tired of being poked and prodded from blood draws and scans, but I never hesitated or delayed those appointments because I realized how important it was to get the cancer out of my body. Sometimes, it took every ounce of strength I had left in my body to go to those appointments, but the relief I felt afterwards in knowing I did everything possible to take care of myself made it all worthwhile.

I did my best to stay strong and be positive each day because it made everyone around me feel better. I couldn't bear the thought of making our young daughter worry more than she was already, and I knew that if I broke down that would put more pressure on Matt to handle the day to day needs of our family. He was already doing so much for us, and I didn't feel as though it would be fair to add to the burden my health had already imposed on him. So, each night after my husband and daughter fell asleep, I laid silently in bed with my eyes open, imagining the worst possible scenarios. The love I feel for my husband and daughter is immeasurable. Sometimes, I don't feel worthy of their immense love and the joy that we soak up together as a family. But my biggest fear is that my greatest loves will be taken away somehow, and cancer provided the perfect weapon.

What if my life is cut short, and I don't get to see my daughter grow up? What if I don't get to see her graduate, fall in love, find her passions, or get married? What if I no longer get to feel my husband's loving arms around me or live out the rest of our dreams together? What if my daughter has to grow up without her Mom? How will Matt handle everything on his own?

These thoughts raced through my mind each night, but I kept them tucked deep inside each day and put on a brave face to keep everyone else from worrying more than they already were. I felt that if I appeared to be strong and unphased, perhaps they would feel that way, too.

The day before my surgery, I set up an email account for our daughter who was eight at the time. I wrote her two emails telling her just how much I loved her, how special she was to me, and I shared some of my thoughts about life. It was pretty painful to write those messages to my daughter, not knowing what the future would hold, but I couldn't bare not having the opportunity to say some of those things to her. I wrote a special card out for Matt and it happened to be Mother's Day so we all spent the day by the pool at a nearby hotel. It was a perfect family day and I did my best not to focus on the future.

Pam offered to stay at our house and watch Zoe while I was in the hospital. She arrived that night, and Zoe ran up to her and said "Aunt Hambone!" and gave her a big hug. They were close and enjoyed making each other laugh. Zoe called her "Aunt Ham" when she was first learning to talk, and then it evolved to "Aunt Hambone", and the name stuck. I was so relieved to see Zoe happy and seemingly unconcerned with my upcoming procedure.

After we turned the lights out that night and crawled into bed, I did my nightly meditation. When it was over and Matt had fallen asleep, I thought about my upcoming surgery and the cancer that was holding my body hostage. For the first time in my life, I felt mortal. I was no longer the invincible woman who paraglided off mountains and rappelled down waterfalls. I was just another wife and mother pleading for more time. Although I was scared, it occurred to me how much I had to be grateful for. I was married to the love of my life, and we had the most amazing, spirited, curly-haired, eight-year-old daughter. I was keenly aware of all the privileges I've had in my life. I've had the opportunity to receive a higher education, travel, and run my own businesses. A deep feeling of peace came over me that night, realizing that I've lived a pretty incredible life. But I wasn't ready for it to be over.

The next morning, Matt and I had to leave around 4:30am to be at the hospital by 5:00am so they could inject blue radioactive dye into the sentinel lymph nodes around my breasts to track the path of my cancer. This procedure is known to be extremely painful and the doctors don't give you pain medicine for it. I was feeling a bit nervous about it, and the biopsy lived up to the hype in the pain department. I was relieved to have it behind me, and I was feeling ready to face the procedure to remove my breasts that was about to happen. I went in for surgery feeling pretty calm and in good spirits, overall. They wheeled me into the Operating Room and all I could think about was how cold it was in there. They talked to me for about two minutes, then I was out. When I woke up in the recovery area, I was so woozy. The room was spinning so fast and I was insanely thirsty.

"Oh okay" was all that I could say for more than an hour.

I motioned for more water, and I drank several large mugs of water and countless spoonfuls of ice before the spinning eased up a bit and they wheeled me into my room. It turns out that thirst and dry mouth are side effects of the anti-nausea patch they administered to stave off any sickness I might have from the anaesthesia.

Matt was waiting for me in the room, and I smiled at him, but all I could say was "I'm so thirsty."

He smiled back at me warmly, and I could tell he was relieved to see that I was okay. I looked down at my chest and noticed my breasts were gone, and all I could see was padding wrapped around my flat chest! This was not what was planned or agreed upon, and nobody warned me that this could be a possible outcome. I was in shock.

Before I had a chance to say anything, my surgeon walked in and explained that they had to abort the plans to do my reconstructive surgery because they found cancer in the other breast and in two of my lymph nodes. It was so obvious that they could see it with their eyes without needing a microscope. This was not what they were expecting either. She explained that it was extremely rare to have the mammogram, ultrasound, and MRI all come back showing that the lymph nodes were clear when cancer was, in fact, in the lymph nodes.

They had to switch gears on the fly during my surgery and decided, without talking to anyone about it, to put tissue expanders inside my breasts because I would probably need radiation. I knew they did the right thing that day, but that didn't make it any easier to process this unexpected turn of events. I trusted them emphatically, my bad-ass team of all women doctors and surgeons were the best in their field and I was so grateful to be in their care, but I was terrified. They told me my cancer was caught early and wasn't in my lymph nodes. How could this be possible? They assured me they would treat me as they would their own Sister or Mom, and that gave me some comfort, but I was rattled. It made me realize when they made the decision to abort the surgery and place the expanders in my chest, that they knew this was more serious. Apparently, radiation would damage the new tissue and they didn't want to ruin my new breasts.

This is much more serious since it's in my lymph nodes, and it means I will need another major surgery down the road. I wasn't prepared for this outcome. I was shaken to my core.

Matt handed me water and ice for a few hours. We didn't really talk about what went wrong or what needed to happen. I was too tired to think about it, and I think he was still processing everything, too. I told him that I would probably go to sleep and he should head home to be there for Zoe. We wanted to maintain as much of a routine for her as possible, and we knew that having Matt at home would help put Zoe's mind at ease.

The next morning, I woke up and went for a walk. Then I went into the restroom, and I pulled the hospital gown aside and removed the padding so I could see what was underneath. I gasped when I saw my deformed body. My breasts were gone, and all that was remaining was red, inflamed, droopy skin with incisions going all the way across both sides of my chest. I looked like a monster or an alien. Every last thread of my femininity felt like it had vanished. I looked like a mutilated boy.

There was a lot to unpack, but there was no time for feeling sorry for myself. Matt and Zoe were on their way to the hospital to pick me up. I needed to pull myself together. When they got there, Zoe was focused on my room and the cool wheelchair I got to sit in on the way down to the car. She didn't seem too worried about me, and I took comfort in that.

For the next ten days, Matt drained my surgical drains a couple times a day and I would take a shower and try to walk around. Overall, the pain wasn't that bad and I only took the prescribed medication for a couple of days, then I took Ibuprofen and Tylenol afterwards.

Matt and I met with my Oncologist a couple weeks after my surgery, and she said the positive lymph nodes were her biggest concern, and she upgraded my cancer to a stage 2B. She explained that my Oncotype DX genomic test scores were really low. Basically, if the scores are low for a tumor, that means chemotherapy would not be significantly beneficial for treating that particular tumor. So, she concluded that I would not need chemotherapy, but I would need six weeks of radiation treatment.

We went home and tried to unpack everything we were told that day. It was a bit disconcerting that chemotherapy was deemed to be an ineffective treatment for my tumors because chemotherapy is a systemic treatment that can kill small traces of cancer that could be lingering in your body. Without it, there would be a risk that small traces of cancer may have already spread through my body. When I asked about that, she said that the hormone blocking medication I would be taking is considered a systemic treatment, although that medication is more designed to prevent a recurrence or reduce the rate of growth in a tumor, not to kill cancer cells.

It occurred to me if I'd received my cancer diagnosis shortly after Mom died, I wouldn't have been capable of handling it. I felt as though I was only being given what I could handle at each moment. Thank goodness I had the strength and clarity I needed to get through the battle and make all the necessary decisions. I was feeling grateful that I had some time to heal from that heartache so I had the mental clarity to deal with this battle. There was sadness in my heart that Mom couldn't be by my side for the journey, but the relief was much stronger that she didn't have to experience it with me. I knew in my heart she wouldn't have been able to handle seeing me battle cancer, and I would have been doing my best to comfort her at every turn.

Matt & I with our 1st place Chili Cook-off trophy, Austin

Modified sign in the Virgin Islands after the 2017 hurricanes.

Pain reaches the heart with electrical speed, but truth moves to the heart as slowly as a glacier. ~Barbara Kingsolver

Burning Body

After my surgical drains were removed, my incredible plastic surgeon Dr. P and her amazing team of PAs and nurses began filling my tissue expanders with saline. Other women who'd been through this procedure warned me that it would really hurt, but it didn't. Strangely, I watched them stick the long needle into the port in my breast, but I didn't feel anything. I had lost all remnants of feeling in my chest area, and the PA told me that most likely I won't ever regain feeling in that area. As she filled my expanders, I felt myself silently begging to feel the pain I'd heard stories about. I just wanted to feel something, but the feeling in my breasts was another piece of my femininity ravaged by this horrible disease. I also lost my nipples. My surgeon told me they would try to save them if they could, but my tumors were too close to the nipple area, so they couldn't be salvaged. I let them know in advance that my health was more important to me than my nipples, so they knew they had my support to remove them if it appeared risky to leave them intact.

When they were filling my expanders, they told me that I had made the right choice to get a double mastectomy. Some women would have opted for the less invasive lumpectomy surgery, but my instincts strongly led me in that direction. I felt there was something in my body that needed to be taken out and I was relieved that they had removed all of that tissue. They could reconstruct my breasts, but the one thing

I feared might be gone forever was my femininity. That wasn't something you could just restore overnight. It's something you feel from the inside and it's either there, or it's not.

Would my husband still find me attractive? Would all of this have an impact on our intimacy? Would we ever be able to get past all of this and feel any sense of normalcy again? I wondered.

Matt reassured me in every way that my health was the most important thing and that he would love me the same with or without my breasts, and I trusted his sincerity. I felt laser-focused on the decisions I needed to make to navigate my way through treatment, and there wasn't much time to over think things at that point. My surgeons submitted my case to a Tumor Board comprised of other surgeons and doctors in the area. They reviewed various cases where a second opinion was needed. She had removed seven lymph nodes during my surgery, but my surgeon wanted to see whether it would be beneficial for me to have another surgery where she could remove more lymph nodes in lieu of radiation. Ultimately, the Board voted unanimously that I should do radiation instead of having more lymph nodes removed, but I had reservations about radiation because it was known to cause secondary cancers, and radiation to the left chest wall can also lead to heart and lung problems.

Two of my best girlfriends, Erin and Lisa, from high school work for a nonprofit called Thrivewell Cancer Foundation in San Antonio. This incredible organization helps people who are battling cancer access the resources they need. I called my friend Erin and explained my diagnosis. It was a powerful conversation between lifelong friends. I had known her since we were in grade school together, and now she was the Executive Director of this amazing foundation. She was able to provide invaluable guidance to me and my family.

She generously offered to have a highly respected Oncologist review the results from my lab tests, and after the physician reviewed them, she agreed that the best next step for treatment of my particular tumors was radiation. That was the additional assurance I needed to move forward with the plan although I was dreading radiation with every fiber of my being. I had heard horror stories of burning skin and future cancer recurrences being caused by all the radiation exposure. I began a ritual of nightly meditations to help ease my anxiety.

I found an incredible Radiation Oncologist with the guidance of my brilliant cousin (and doctor) Leigh. She helped me locate a doctor who used the Deep Inspiration Breath Hold (DIBH) technique, often used in conjunction with left chest wall radiation to minimize risk to the heart and lungs. Before my first treatment, they had to deflate my right breast tissue expander because they were worried it would get in the way. So, that left me with one filled breast and one flat breast. As it turned out, the only thing that felt worse than having no breasts was having only one.

I was scheduled for twenty-eight radiation sessions. I drove nearly an hour each way five days a week for about a month and a half. After radiation, I went to the gym and got on the treadmill, then I went to Juiceland and ordered a green juice. I was on auto-pilot. My husband wanted to come with me to these appointments, but we decided that he needed to be there to take Zoe to and from school and he was the only one working and bringing in an income at the time. We couldn't afford to lose that security, especially with everything we were already facing. Also, I explained to him that visitors were not allowed to come into the treatment rooms, so it was really something I needed to do alone. He got me a subscription to Sirius radio to enjoy during my drives, and I listened to my favorite podcasts. That really helped to ease my anxiety during that time.

One of the biggest challenges during radiation was the fatigue and missing out on all of the summer fun taking place around us. Our local friends and neighbors spent weekday evenings and weekends on the lake or by the pool. Since we had a young daughter at home, we didn't want to deprive her of that time with her friends, so we took her to the pool or lake early in the morning or late in the evening, and I stayed in the shade and out of the water. I struggled with feelings of guilt for not being the mom Zoe may have wanted at the time. I longed to be in the water playing with her, but it just wasn't possible that summer. I didn't like to complain, so I held in my frustration with not being able to do those things outside.

My sweet friend and neighbor Nicole could really see me and the struggle I was going through, so she offered to meet up with me in the evenings so our kids could play together while we sat by the pool and visited. Those moments allowed me to maintain a somewhat normal life for my daughter and also allowed me an opportunity to get outside. I really needed those moments to help me get through a difficult time. We had lots of great family and friends who brought us meals and dropped by to see us at the house, and I will be forever grateful for their love and support. But those summer evenings sitting by the pool with Nicole and her family helped keep my spirits up by providing an ounce of normalcy during an otherwise dark time.

The radiation treatment itself wasn't too painful for the first few weeks, but by the time I reached the last couple weeks of treatment, I had severe, blistering burns across my left breast, under my left arm and on my back like an exit wound. It was so painful, and the skin was breaking down and oozing. I wasn't sure I could get across the finish line.

I met with my Radiation Oncologist one day and told her, in tears, that I wasn't sure I could continue. It was so hard to continue burning my body when it had already burnt that badly. She prescribed me a special cream and told me how research showed if you take a break between radiation treatments that it can impact rates of recurrence. So, I summoned all of my strength and I finished my treatments. It felt incredible to be finished with that milestone. Matt insisted on coming with me to my last treatment, and my treatment team had me ring a bell and they gave me a certificate of completion for radiation.

We booked a trip to Kauai to celebrate the milestones of completing my double mastectomy and radiation as well as our wedding anniversary. We took Zoe with us because we knew how much she would love Kauai from our previous visits there. We had a spectacular trip. We splurged on a helicopter trip over the island and we snorkeled and hiked and ate poke and fresh fruit. I was allowed to swim for the first time in months, and it felt breath-taking to be in the ocean, free floating with my husband and our daughter after everything I'd just been through.

We returned from that trip and I began to feel stronger. The holidays were coming and we planned lots of family activities to celebrate together. I was so grateful to be with my family. My doctors told me I had to wait a minimum of four months after radiation for my reconstructive surgery, so we scheduled it for exactly that time.

My birthday came around and normally we would have a simple dinner to celebrate. This time around, however, was very different. We heard that Jimmy Fallon was coming to Austin to film the Tonight Show at the University of Texas. On my actual birthday. Matt and I made a pact that we would get tickets for the show. The trouble was that tickets were only available for currently enrolled students at UT. We sent a letter to the university asking if we could volunteer for the event, and we shared that UT was my alma mater and that I was currently undergoing treatment for breast cancer. We were wondering if there was any way we could help out during the event so there might be an opportunity to see the show, too. We received a nice letter back from the President's Office saying they didn't need any more volunteers, but they wanted to offer us two complimentary tickets to the show!

The night of the show, we arrived early to get in line, and Matthew McConaughey drove past us, riding in the back of a SUV. He rolled the window down and gave us a "Hook

'Em" sign. Then, he got out and walked around the back of the building. The excitement was building. We finally made our way inside for the show and the Roots sang Happy Birthday to a few of us who had birthdays that day, before the show began. Chip and Joanna Gaines were on the show, too. We had an incredible night, but we were feeling pretty tired after such a big day.

When the show was over, we went over to a quaint little restaurant away from campus for a relaxing dinner. We had one of the best meals I can remember, then as we were leaving, we noticed that Chip & Joanna Gaines were at the same restaurant and getting ready to leave at the same time.

As we walked by we said "We really enjoyed the show tonight!" They graciously chatted with us for a while, and they were incredibly down to earth and charming. We told them we were celebrating my birthday and that I just finished radiation treatment for breast cancer.

Chip looked at me and said "You are going to beat this!" I knew at that moment that I would never have another birthday like that again. I was fully soaking up each moment of the wild ride that my life had become.

Tara and Megan offered to fly to Austin for a girl's weekend and I was moved to tears with excitement over the thought of spending a carefree weekend with two of my best girlfriends in the world. They first met when Tara came to visit me in San Francisco and they saw each other again at our wedding, so they knew each other pretty well. Megan and I worked together in San Francisco at the online wine company, and we had remained close. She has great comedic timing, and she was excited for a fun girls' weekend. She has teenage twins with her husband in Ann Arbor, and she is an elementary school teacher. Tara had been my soul sister for decades, and she flew in from San Diego. The girls arrived on Thursday night and stayed until Sunday. We had the best time together and filled the weekend with plenty of adventures. We went on a bike ride and explored the River Walk in San Antonio where we enjoyed great Mexican food.

Then we hiked to the top of Enchanted Rock in Fredericksburg, and we went to a local winery on our way back to Austin. Time flew by too quickly, but we were able to catch up and share plenty of laughs during their visit. Something as simple as a relaxed weekend with two of my closest friends did wonders for my mental health. I hadn't realized until they got there just how much I needed a break from thinking about cancer.

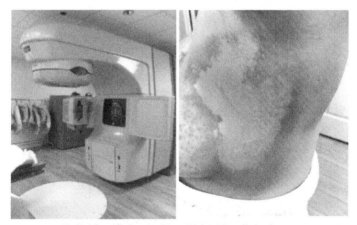

(Left): The radiation machine. (Right): My radiation burns.

(Above): Tara, Me, & Megan

True self-care is not salt baths and chocolate, it is making the choice to build a life you don't need to regularly escape from. ~Brianna Wiest

Dumpster Fire

Before too long, Christmas arrived. We got a big tree and we did all the holiday rituals together as a family. We had to work almost every day that month, but I was just grateful to have my family by my side to enjoy this special occasion together. For New Years Eve, our amazing neighbors were going to be celebrating across the street with a fun house party, but we decided we wanted to spend that night with our daughter. It had been such a big and challenging year and we wanted to include her in the celebrations of not only a new year, but a new decade. We rented a hotel room in downtown Austin and we swam in the rooftop pool and watched fireworks, full of hope for the future.

Two weeks later, Matt's Mom (Gramma D) flew in to watch Zoe for us while I was in the hospital for my breast reconstruction surgery. This time, I was scheduled to stay in the hospital for several days after the surgery since it was such a big procedure. The surgery could last up to twelve or thirteen hours, but my surgeon was so fantastic that she was normally able to do it in about half that time if there were no complications. Gramma D is wonderful with Zoe, so it was reassuring to have her there to help our daughter and also to be there for Matt. He was going to have his hands full visiting me in the hospital, dealing with urgent work issues, and caring for me after I got home from the hospital. He said he could handle it all, but I felt much happier and more at ease having his Mom there with us while I was in the hospital and home recovering.

I felt pretty calm and relaxed going into surgery, but I realized the magnitude of the procedure. It felt a little easier knowing that the surgery would be focused on giving me new breasts instead of pathology. When I came out of the operating room, I felt much better than I did after the double mastectomy. The room wasn't spinning as badly, although I was still really thirsty. When the nurse was wheeling me into my room after surgery, she told Matt that I had been rapping and singing things like "the left side is the best side" and laughing about everything. He wasn't too surprised. They put me in a room that was set aside for patients who need hourly care. The nurses in that area have been trained to deal with patients who have been through breast reconstruction, so they were prepared to place the doppler ultrasound on my chest every hour to check for blood flow. On the morning of my second day recovering in the hospital, they told me something was wrong with my lungs. When they tried to reduce the supplemental oxygen they were giving me to wean me off after the surgery, my oxygen levels plummeted. They couldn't figure out why they couldn't get my oxygen levels to stabilize, but that continued to be an issue for the next few days, and I was experiencing strong chest pain on the right side. I got up and walked around and eventually they got my oxygen levels to stabilize enough to release me. Matt, Zoe, Gramma D, and Aunt Pam all came to the hospital to visit and take me home, and I was on top of the world to have that surgery behind me. The comfort I found in safely arriving home was immeasurable. I wore my own soft pajamas, and I was surrounded by family and free of IVs and beeping machines. It felt like paradise at the time.

Matt was a seasoned pro at handling my surgical drains, so twice a day he removed everything from the drains and measured the fluids. I was ready to have my drains removed in just two days. We were both thrilled to hear I was able to get them out so quickly. I had to keep the drains in longer after my double mastectomy, and this had been a much longer and more involved surgery. We were ecstatic with the good news.

Even though Matt was very sweet and patient helping me with the drains each day, I was painfully aware of what an unpleasant task that was, and I was so eager for both of us to get back to our normal routines. I had to use a walker for a few weeks after my surgery before I was allowed to stand upright and walk on my own again. It took about three full months for the chest pain and shortness of breath to subside, but eventually everything healed. My abdominal incision goes from the middle of one side of my hip all the way across to the middle of the other side of my hip. I have new breasts now and they look pretty damn good for an almost fifty-year old woman. When I'm feeling fancy, I even put on my prosthetic nipples. They are incredibly realistic and definitely help me feel fully like myself again. The breast reconstruction procedure was anything but easy, but I am relieved to feel like I have my femininity back, so the whole process feels worthwhile.

For a while, it felt good to just put life on hold and recover. About a month after my surgery, Coronavirus began spreading rampantly through the country, and businesses (including ours) shuttered down and all the schools in our area closed. We took that time as an opportunity to rest and recover more so I could fully heal and recharge my batteries from everything my body had been through, and we all needed to catch our breath from the grueling year we had just been through. We were forced to stop working and socializing, so that allowed us more time at home as a family. To say that being locked inside your home with a nine year old for months on end is challenging is a serious understatement. We love our daughter and her outgoing and feisty personality, but children aren't meant to be locked inside for long periods of time with their parents. It makes everyone feel crazy.

We must not have had enough struggle for a while because things in our lives were about to get even more challenging.

Zoe tested positive for Strep, and a few days after she finished her antibiotics she began clearing her throat incessantly. This became so constant that we grew concerned, then we noticed that she was also twitching her head, and she couldn't seem to control that either. We asked her pediatrician about this, but they blew it off and said to give it some time and it should resolve on its own. So, we sought the help of a Naturopath and Nutritionist. They insisted that we have a GI-Map test done with a stool sample that was supposed to shed some light on what is going on with her digestive system. It turned out that Zoe had some extensive bacterial and parasitic infections. She also had strep bacteria remaining in her body.

After more extensive testing, they told us that our daughter had PANDAS (Pediatric Autoimmune Neuropsychiatric Disorders Associated with Streptococcal Infections). Apparently, the strep bacteria survive in the body by hiding from the immune system by putting molecules on their cell wall so they look like molecules found on the child's brain tissue. So, when the immune system detects a problem and produces antibodies, those antibodies often attack the child's brain tissue that looks the same as the bacteria that is camouflaged nearby. When this happens, children often display tics, OCD behaviors, anxiety, moodiness, and separation anxiety.

Basically, that was just enough to put us over the edge into the dumpster fire that 2020 had become and we could no longer deny it. It was a shit-storm and it felt like we were stuck in the eye of it. For the next two and a half months, we gave Zoe a cocktail of horrid tasting medicine that was prescribed to eradicate these predators from her body. The doctors also said we needed to put her on a gluten free, sugar free and dairy free diet while we were treating her. The only thing worse than imprisoning a young child for months on end in your home is to completely restrict all the foods they love and fill them with awful tasting medicine each day. Nobody prepared us for how difficult the detox process would be. Zoe had massive panic attacks that made her feel like she couldn't breathe and she was really nauseous. These attacks struck at all hours of the day and night, so none of us were sleeping much. After we got through the worst of her treatment, we were shell-shocked. We felt like the hits just kept coming, and we were in search of a better path for our family.

We began having discussions about how we'd lost our edge, and we were brainstorming ways to reclaim it and find joy in our daily lives again. We immediately reflected on how happy we felt in Kauai. We were so in awe of the beauty of the island and its healing qualities that we had decided a while back to do everything we could to retire there one day. After my Cancer treatment, Zoe's illness, and a global pandemic, it became crystal clear to us that our future wasn't guaranteed.

Why should we wait until after we retired to pursue a dream that we knew would make us happier now? That question resonated with us for the next couple of months.

We weighed our options carefully. In the end, we decided that Hawaii was a place that could offer us a healthier, happier, simpler life, so we decided to put our house on the market in Austin to see if it would sell. Then, we would just let things play out organically. We got an offer on the first day.

Me hiking the Kalalau Trail, Kauai 2005

Twenty years from now you will be more disappointed by the things that you didn't do than by the ones you did do. So throw off the bowlines. Sail away from the safe harbor. Catch the trade winds in your sails. ~H. Jackson Brown, Jr.

Across the Pacific

When we got the offer on our house, we were shocked and terrified.

What had we done? Reality was setting in and we had to make a decision about whether we were ready to make the move. We talked about it and slept on it. We only have one life, and we were determined to make the most of ours, but the stakes were so high for our daughter. Her happiness means the world to us. We were definitely ready to chase our bliss and find our edge that we'd somehow lost after we sold our zipline business and Mom died. Our favorite memories as a family were living by the ocean in Alaska and Washington. We were dreaming of finding our passions again-swimming, surfing, snorkeling, paddle-boarding, fishing and boating. We felt that Hawaii could provide some things for our daughter that would be a challenge to find in the Lower 48. We were in search of a simpler life where materialism wasn't the focus and family values were more important. We found a small school that focused on outdoor education. Anxiety was a concern for all of us, and we felt like the slower pace of island time would be a healthy change for everyone. There is research that shows the ocean has therapeutic qualities. It has healing powers for stress and anxiety. We believed that Kauai would provide a healthier lifestyle for us because it has an abundance of fresh fruit, vegetables and fish. "Island time" is a real thing in Hawaii where people don't get stressed about doing anything in a hurry. The weather is nice enough year-round that you can be active outside every day.

The only things holding us back from moving to Hawaii were the fear of how the move would impact our daughter and what others would think of us. Our good friends always joke with us that we move as frequently as a military family. We realized that some of our friends and family thought our transient lifestyle was crazy, but we were in agreement that the only opinions that mattered on this topic were ours.

But I definitely paused to consider why I was always moving from one place to another so freely, wearing a new town like the next black dress in my closet. *What was I running from?* I wondered. *Was I trying to escape or avoid confronting something?* The psychologist in me was sure there was something deeper going on. I had been a nomad most of my life, but I had grown tired of that lifestyle. Matt and I had happily floated from place to place over the years, but now we had a child to consider. We had become painfully aware of the burden our wanderlust was putting on our daughter.

We decided that Zoe was getting old enough that her opinion needed to be considered, so we decided to talk to her about the idea of moving to Hawaii. She was an ocean girl at heart and she was the first to say that. She loved swimming, snorkeling and looking for underwater creatures more than anything else. But she had spent the past three formative years of her life making friends and visiting family, and we knew that meant a lot to her. When we first mentioned it to her, she said she didn't want to move. There were tears shed, and we listened to her carefully and let her express her feelings openly. We told her that she had a vote in this decision and we cared how she felt. We explained the pros and cons as we saw them. Eventually, she told us she wanted to go, but part of her wanted to stay at the same time. Matt and I sifted through her comments and did our best to assess what would be best for our little family.

We temporarily accepted the offer on our house, but we agreed to take more time to see if Zoe was really onboard with the move before we finalized anything. There would be an opportunity to change our minds. We took Zoe on hikes and bike rides in the days that followed. We let her speak freely about her feelings. At first, she was too sad about leaving her friends to feel good about the move.

Then, a couple days later she said that she would rather live in Hawaii near the ocean and marine life, but she was just struggling with leaving her friends. We told her that we understood and explained that we would definitely come back to visit because we have family and friends in Texas. That seemed to seal the deal for her. If we could live in Hawaii but come back to visit, that was a plan she could get her head around. So, we continued moving forward.

My Oncologist explained that the last step in my cancer treatment, aside from the estrogen blocking medication I will take for ten years, was to have my ovaries removed. Since my breast cancer was estrogen-fed, one of the most important treatments they recommend is removing the estrogen from its source: the ovaries. I had also struggled with endometriosis most of my life, so my Oncologist suggested a total hysterectomy. I found a fantastic surgeon, Dr. K, who specializes in laparoscopic hysterectomies. She quickly squeezed me into her calendar, even in the midst of the global pandemic.

Due to Coronavirus (COVID) and the stay-home restrictions that were in place, we couldn't have any family come stay with us to help out for this surgery. So, the plan was that I would drive myself to the hospital and check in for surgery early that morning, and Matt would take Zoe to horse camp, then he would come check on me at the hospital.

First, I had to drive across town and take a COVID test. I had to prove that I was COVID-free before I could be cleared for surgery. I pulled up to the entrance of the hospital, and nurses in protective gear and face shields were greeting the car in front of me. I followed the written instructions and put my face mask on, turned my car off and rolled my windows down. It was over a hundred degrees outside, and I was sweating like crazy in my mask, waiting for about twenty minutes for my turn. The woman in the car in front of me screamed when they put the swab up her nose.

"Oh shit" I said audibly.

How bad could a nose swab really be? I wondered.

The nurse came over to me and instructed me to put my head up against my headrest, then she proceeded to jam the long swab so far up my nose that I could only see the tip sticking out.

"Ow!" I yelped, equal parts annoyed and embarrassed.

She pulled the swab out and there was blood on it. I had been through so many harder things over the past year, but sometimes it's that one small thing that puts you over the edge. I wasn't in the mood for it that day. I'd had enough already. My test results came back negative, and I was cleared for surgery.

By a stroke of luck, my surgery was delayed and Matt was able to get to the hospital in time to see me before they wheeled me into the OR that I'd become intimately familiar with over the past year and a half. I was under anaesthesia in a couple minutes and the surgery lasted less than one hour. It was a cake-walk compared to my other surgeries. Dr. K said that it was standard protocol to stay at least one night in the hospital after the surgery because it was a pretty major procedure, but I felt really good when I got out of recovery so she agreed to let me go home the same day to be with my family.

One of the biggest challenges we faced with our move during COVID was that flights were being cancelled and rules for travel were frequently changing. We were planning to bring Mariposa because she was an important part of our family, but the logistics were challenging.

In order to bring our dog to Hawaii, we had to file tons of paperwork, get special blood tests for rabies antibodies, pay all sorts of fees and get check-ups just before our departure. Those things were always required for people to bring dogs into Hawaii. Since COVID was also an issue, there was a moratorium on pet travel to Hawaii. The only exception the state would consider was for service animals. So, I contacted a therapist and explained the anxiety I had been experiencing since my treatment and Zoe's illness, and he said I definitely qualified to have an emotional support dog. He wrote me a letter of support, and we submitted that paperwork to the airlines and the state of Hawaii for approval.

The last couple weeks in our house were a huge push to sell most of our belongings and pack everything that remained into a small pod that we would later have shipped to Hawaii once we were settled. The condo we rented for our first few months in Hawaii was furnished, so we really didn't need much in the immediate future. I think it was hard for Zoe to watch all of our things disappearing, and she was dreading saying goodbye to her friends. We couldn't have a real going-away party because of COVID, so we distantly said goodbye outside the house to our closest family and friends before we left on our journey for Hawaii.

We were on the road for three long days before arriving in Los Angeles. While we were there, we got a health certificate for our dog, loaded some of our belongings onto the barge for Hawaii, and shipped our vehicles. We only had a few days to do all of that and visit a few of our closest friends in the area. Finally, the moment we were planning for was upon us. We were getting closer to realizing our dreams if we could just get through the move.

In Honolulu, we had to get an inspection for Mariposa, then we caught our flight to Kauai. Finally, we arrived. We'd never experienced such a challenging move in our lives, not even driving through the blizzard to Alaska pulling a pontoon boat. We were experienced movers, but this one had been a real doozy. We walked outside onto the balcony overlooking the stunning crystal blue ocean and stood in silence together for several moments. I think we were quietly wondering if our new surroundings would bring us the joy and inspiration we were so desperately pursuing. This was the moment we had all worked so hard for and it definitely felt good, but we needed to recharge a bit to fully process it.

We survived mom's passing, moving across the country twice (including once across the Pacific Ocean), breast cancer, our daughter's PANDAS diagnosis, and a global pandemic over the course of the past five years. We were feeling ready for less adversity and more joy in the years to come.

(Left): Zoe & Mariposa. (Right): At the beach Kauai, HI.

(Left):Mariposa on a walk during quarantine. (Right): Our ohana (family).

They asked me what I wanted to be when I grew up. I wrote down 'happy'. They told me I didn't understand the assignment, and I told them they didn't understand life. ~John Lennon

Reckoning

We purchased a quaint little farmhouse in Kauai, and once we settled in, I finally had an opportunity to reflect back on my life. A cancer diagnosis has a way of illuminating everything and bringing all the truth to the surface. As your fate hangs in the balance, you quickly sort out what matters and rings true from the bullshit that doesn't deserve your limited time and energy.

I was sitting on the lanai drinking a cup of Kona coffee one morning when I was hit with the realization that all the cross-country moves and entrepreneurial adventures that shaped my life were not solely driven by moxie and grit. My nomadic lifestyle had been an escape route that enabled me to avoid reckoning with my past trauma, grief, and anxiety. This realization crashed over me like a tsunami wave.

How could a grown-ass woman with a graduate degree in Psychology not have picked up on such an obvious pattern? I wondered.

As I took in this information, I felt physically ill. I had the urge to vomit, but instead I put my bathing suit on and headed straight to the ocean for a long, hard swim. I had to release some endorphins and breathe so that I could handle the staggering emotions I was feeling.

I'd stored my pain, anxiety, and grief under layers of skin as if they'd perhaps be useful to me sometime in the future, like a bear who packs on pounds for hibernation. Cancer had split me wide open, and all the buried pain began to ooze to the surface. Finally, I faced my pain head-on, and I was able to work through and release it. It felt so liberating to finally tackle this internal beast I'd spent a lifetime running from.

I'm now able to see this troubling pattern with haunting clarity. When life has thrown curveballs my way, I've almost always flown the coop. Instead of pausing to feel the pain and examine the problems that have surfaced in my life, I've upped the ante and pursued greater challenges that adequately kept me busy and distracted me from feeling grief, disappointment, and loss. I would never suggest that my path of going big in the face of adversity is better than alternate routes, but for better or worse, it's what I've done my entire life. It can be exhausting at times, but if I am handed lemons, I'll find a way to make some damn lemonade.

I spent the better part of a month walking, swimming, and crying. Crying is an extremely healthy outlet, but I've never been very good at allowing my emotions to rise to the surface. It was so liberating to be able to cry and release years of pain and grief that were stuck deep below the surface. I knew this reckoning was inevitable and needed to happen so I could move forward with my life in a healthier, more authentic way.

I gave a lot of thought to what caused my cancer, and my instincts told me that all of the trauma and struggle in my life may have contributed to my health challenges somehow. Stress and childhood trauma can be woven into the fabric of our being. Therapy, journaling, exercise, and meditation can be useful tools for healing, but often those threads remain within us. I would be naïve to think that those things didn't contribute to my illness in any way.

Harvard Health Publishing released an article in February of 2019 entitled "Past trauma may haunt your future health" explaining how adverse childhood experiences can impact our future health and risk for diseases like cancer. When you experience something that provokes heightened anxiety, your body produces more adrenaline, and your heart rate normally goes up. "This wear and tear on your body ages your system faster" and increases inflammation as a result. Heightened inflammation levels have been associated with many diseases, including cancer.

A year prior to my diagnosis, I wasn't feeling well, so I went to my general practitioner for a check-up. She performed a blood test, and the results came back showing high levels of inflammation and low pH levels. Inflammation and an acidic pH may not directly cause cancer, but both of them create an environment in our bodies that is hospitable to diseases such as cancer. I asked my doctor what I could do to improve those levels, and she didn't really have any advice for me. One year later, I was diagnosed with cancer. I'm not trying to suggest that these things directly caused my cancer, but research has shown there is a connection, and I hope that sharing my experience with others will help raise awareness and hopefully encourage others to focus on prevention and improve their overall health. More research needs to be done to further explore the connection between stress, childhood trauma, inflammation, and cancer. If you have cancer, it's important to follow your Oncologist's recommendations for treatment. It may also be helpful to get blood tests that check your inflammation and pH levels so you can do everything possible to improve your overall health and reduce your risk of recurrence.

Another factor that may have contributed to my cancer diagnosis is dense breast tissue. Dense breasts have large amounts of glandular tissue and fibrous connective tissue and relatively low amounts of fatty breast tissue. Dense breasts are fairly common as nearly half of women over the age of forty who receive mammograms have them. I found out that I had very dense breast tissue after receiving my first few mammograms. I asked what that meant, and I was simply told that it means that sometimes it can be harder to detect tumors through mammograms when a person has dense breasts. I asked if I could receive 3D mammograms since they are supposed to be more accurate with finding cancer in dense breast tissue, but my insurance company wouldn't cover the procedure. I often wonder if my cancer may have been found earlier if I had been able to receive 3D mammograms. Of course, there is no way to know for sure, but I have found out by doing my own research that breast cancer is more common in people with dense breast tissue. None of my doctors or technicians mentioned this fact to me. Had I known, I would have definitely pushed harder to receive 3D mammograms, even if I had to come up with the additional money out of pocket. I would recommend that all women over the age of forty find out whether you have dense breast tissue. If you do have it, you may want to have a discussion with your doctor to see if a 3D mammogram or ultrasound would be right for you since they can sometimes be more effective at finding tumors in dense breast tissue.

Breast cancer certainly shaped my life in many significant ways, but I'm determined not to allow it to define my life. One positive impact cancer has had on me is it took me on an unlikely path to find self-love. Somehow, this horrible disease managed to sucker punch me into prioritizing myself. It's difficult to survive cancer if you don't recognize your value and make yourself a priority.

I spent decades putting everyone else's needs and opinions before my own, but I'm done with that now. I finally recognize that I deserve to carve out the time necessary to improve my health and well-being and rest when I feel like it. I told Zoe about my diagnosis and treatments instead of shielding her from it. Having that conversation with her was one of the hardest things I had to do, but I know she'll be stronger for it in the end, and she will be more prepared to handle life's inevitable struggles. I'm learning how to lean into my feelings instead of burying and running from them. It's not easy for me to change that old coping mechanism, but I'm able to relax and enjoy the present moment more when I'm not always looking ahead, planning my next escape route.

I was able to share my feelings of abandonment with my Dad, and we've developed a solid, trusting friendship that is buoyed by reciprocal patience and unconditional love. I made peace with what happened in the past, and I've realized that it's easier to maintain a healthy relationship with him if I release any thoughts or expectations about what the dynamic should be. He lives in the picturesque village of Interlaken, in the mountainous Bernese Oberland region of Switzerland with a music recording studio in his house. We keep in touch and have occasional visits, and that works well for us.

I do everything I can to keep Mom's memory alive. Zoe and I cook some of her favorite recipes together, and that's a great way to stay connected with her. We went out to the ocean to release her ashes, and we always say that the brightest star in the sky is Mom looking down on us.

I'm not entirely sure what my future holds, but I know one thing is true; I won't let fear dictate my choices. I still struggle with anxiety as I continue to feel new aches and see new spots appear on my skin. I'm haunted by the fear of recurrence every single day. Most people don't realize that once you complete cancer treatment, the worrying doesn't stop. It's a lifelong battle as you have ongoing appointments with your Oncologist, and they do scans and blood tests to see if they cancer has returned. I also lose sleep worrying about whether my husband finds this new version of me attractive. The giant scar across my abdomen and across my breasts are a constant reminder of the battle I've been through, and the light-hearted intimacy of our youth has been forever stolen from us. The hormone blocking medication that I have to take for ten years causes hot flashes, horrible neuropathy that causes insomnia, weight gain, bone density loss, severe joint pain, and hair loss. Before my diagnosis, I still felt youthful but now I find myself limping around and asking for help opening jars. I feel as though I've aged at warp speed. I am still mourning all that I've lost, but I finally realized that I am a Warrior, and I've been in training since the day I was born. Everything I've weathered over the course of my life helped me develop into the woman I am today and gave me the strength to fight cancer. The circuitous path I've taken to get to this point hasn't been easy or logical, but I wouldn't change it for anything in the world because each struggle I faced and mistake I've made along the way has made me tougher. I have good days and bad days, just like everyone else, but my self-love and gratitude have grown in ways I never dreamed possible. I feel so much joy in the simple pleasures of everyday life- holding the hands of my loved ones, sharing a cup of coffee with my husband, watching the sunset, and seeing our daughter grow into the remarkable person she is becoming. I feel like a flower slowly making my way up through the hardened, dehydrated caliche of the desert.

I'm slowly gaining momentum and recently started a business focusing on natural wellness. We are doing our best to put down some roots and bloom where we're planted for a change. I made a promise to myself when I was going through treatment that if I made it through the other side, I would do my best to help others who are on a similar journey, and that is my hope with this book and my new business.

Our days often end with a hike, swim or paddle as we watch the sun melt into the ocean. Zoe is really thriving. She's made some great friends, and she is part of a surf club that meets twice a week. Surfing seems to help ease her anxiety, and it's her greatest joy. Recently, we were walking back from the beach, and she was carrying her surfboard on top of her head, barefoot.

She said "Mom, I can't believe we really get to live here." I find solace in knowing that Zoe is already on the path of discovering her passions.

Matt is fully engulfed with farm life. He uses his machete to create trails through the tall grass around our property, and he spends his days trimming trees and putting in fences to keep the wild pigs at bay so we can begin planting our crops. He spends his free time surfing, paddle-boarding, and fishing. We've come to a beautiful place in our relationship where we are more aware than ever of each other's needs, and we do our best to nurture them.

Gradually, I'm prioritizing myself and pursuing my own interests. I'm helping maintain the farm, and when I have a hard day, I find comfort in going for long ocean swims or paddle-boarding with my family to work out the kinks. When I fall, I pull myself back up and try again. Sometimes, I get pulled out by a riptide, and I try to remember to stay calm and know that I'm not going to drown. Eventually, I make my way back to land, and the air tastes sweeter and the colors of the sky are more magnificent the more I had to overcome to reach the shore. I've found my edge again, and a deep feeling of peace has unfurled in my heart. All the struggles I've endured to get to this moment feel worthwhile.

If you don't know what your passion is, realize the one reason for your existence on earth is to find it. ~Oprah Winfrey

Epilogue
(Finding Your Edge)

Living a passionate life doesn't just magically happen; it typically requires a lot of effort to build the life you want instead of just living out the one you're given. It can be a little frustrating when people say "you're so lucky to have your own business", or "things just seem to come easily for you." Honestly, nothing could be farther from the truth. It took so much sacrifice, failure, and persistence to get where I am today. It has been so challenging at times that I didn't know if I could push through and keep going. Not one thing has ever been handed to me, and everything I've earned has been built through an enormous amount of persistence and determination. Opportunities don't just get handed to most of us for no reason. We have to work hard and grind for them, and when we fail, we need to get back up and try again. First, I would like to fully acknowledge how difficult it can be to find the inspiration to make a change in our lives. Sometimes, it feels like just surviving is enough. After I completed treatment for cancer, I found myself stuck in a rut. I was transfixed with worry that cancer was still lingering in my body.

How can I be sure they got it all? That thought plagued my mind day and night, and I was stuck in the pattern of living like the sick person I'd become since my diagnosis. I couldn't figure out how to transition back into living my life with passion again. Finally, I addressed my concerns with my Oncologist. Nobody ever said the words "You are cancer-free" to me after my treatment was complete, so I was living in fear that I still had cancer. He explained that I no longer had cancer, and I could officially move forward with living my life. Those words were like a permission slip for me to chase my dreams again.

There are a variety of ways we find our edge in life-a path that inspires us and makes us truly happy- but it will probably take some grit and courage to get there. One thing that helped me find the motivation to pursue my passions again was to think about how my daughter will remember me when I'm gone. I don't want her to remember me as someone who took risks and accomplished great things before cancer but quit living her life with the same enthusiasm afterwards. I chased some big dreams when I was younger, but I've finally realized that my story doesn't have to be over yet. Hopefully I still have some good years ahead of me, and I really want to make them count.

Perhaps there's a different path out there that would bring you more happiness. What do you want your metaphorical tombstone to say? Do you want to go back to school to pursue an old dream you've given up on, or go after a career in music or art that you lost sight of due to fear of failure? How can you find your edge? Your aspirations may not seem practical and other people may think you're crazy, but if your passions bring you joy and light you up, that's all that really matters. Your happiness shouldn't hurt anyone. You should never have to apologize to anyone for chasing your dreams and finding your edge.

Before you can really pursue a joyful life, it's important to address any obstacles that might be in your way. I was living a very fulfilling life before cancer, but I now realize that I was allowing my adventurous life to distract me from dealing with some lingering pain and grief I hadn't fully resolved. If you feel like there is anything internally standing in the way of your pursuit of real happiness, I recommend addressing it directly first instead of running from it like I did. I feel free of that baggage now that I've processed it and more able to experience authentic happiness than ever before.

I encourage you to begin the process by doing some soul-searching to determine if you are passionate about your life. Do you get out of bed, eager to embrace each day, or do you dreadfully hit the snooze button? Are you excited to talk about things that light you up, or do you feel uninspired? Those are just a couple things to think about to help you determine if you've found your edge. When you are doing something you're passionate about, it feels like there's nothing else you would rather be doing.

For some people, doing work that you're passionate about isn't really an option. Perhaps the work that you most enjoy doing doesn't sufficiently pay the bills. In that case, I would encourage you to really focus on developing hobbies that you're passionate about. Maybe you were into mountain biking or painting when you were younger, but you abandoned those interests when you got married and had kids. It's never too late to pick those things back up again. You owe it to yourself to pursue hobbies that light you up. You'll be happier, and most likely, you'll become a better partner and parent to those you love when your own needs are being met. There's something about a person who is living a passionate life that's contagious. Your joy can be infectious to those around you. If you're needing a little inspiration in your life, pursuing a hobby is a great place to begin.

Your surroundings can also be a great source of inspiration. Some people can find happiness in any location. I admire those people because it's much easier to find contentment without trotting across the globe. But for those of us who thrive on finding inspiration in our surroundings, sometimes we can find our edge simply by choosing to live in an inspirational place. I don't recommend moving every time you're in need of inspiration, but sometimes a small move to a new place can help provide the inspiration you need to get out of a rut. For example, if you're living in a densely populated city, and you love to hike and bike, perhaps just moving to another area of the same city that has more hiking and biking trails could provide the inspiration you need to live a more passionate life. Of course, it's important to balance the needs of your family and career, but if it's possible to do your work in a more inspirational place that would allow you to find your edge, that could be a life-changing move. Alternately, something as simple as a weekend camping trip can be so invigorating. Sometimes, a little retreat into nature with fresh air is all we need to find a new perspective and bring some joy back into our lives.

Living a passionate life isn't easy, and it takes mindfulness to ensure that you don't lose sight of it. I worked hard to find my edge when I was younger, and I was living a passionate life for many years, but I got off track after we sold our zipline business, Mom died, and I was diagnosed with cancer. I'm so grateful I finally came to the realization that my story didn't have to end with cancer. I was eager to get back to following my heart again and living a more passionate life once my cancer treatment was complete. I signed up for an online workshop aimed at helping clients get out of a rut and taking action to live their best lives. After completing that workshop, I found the motivation I needed to move to a place that inspired me, finish writing this book, and hopefully help other people who've experienced similar struggles.

I'm so grateful to feel like I finally have my edge back! I've finally discovered, after a lifetime of bouncing around, that living a life of passion doesn't have to involve extreme sports and international travel. I'm gradually coming to terms with the reality that it's possible to live an adventurous life exactly where I am without pushing my limits beyond the breaking point. In fact, a large part of my own journey to happiness has been internal. It's difficult to live an authentically joyful life if the happiness is only derived from external things. It takes a culmination of internal peace and doing what you love to really find authentic happiness.

Finding your edge and living a life of passion is enormously beneficial because it blows the wind into your sails and builds your confidence so you can more adequately handle life's inevitable challenges. When you're buoyed up with the joy and satisfaction of doing things that make you happy, it's much easier to weather the obstacles that will be thrown your way. Life is too short to waste it worrying about things we can't control. It's much easier to focus on the things you can improve and let go of things that are beyond your reach.

I believe that helping to coach our children to find their passions from a young age is one of the greatest gifts we can give them. It's not our job to determine or influence what their passions might be, but we can help them explore possibilities and be in tune with them so we can recognize the signs when we see them light up doing something they truly love. If kids are able to identify their passions from a young age, it can help give their life purpose and keep them from feeling emptiness and lack of belonging. If they have passions that keep them motivated and fulfilled, they won't be looking for other things to fill that void.

I encourage you to make a list of the top ten things you really want to do with your one precious life. This could be a fun exercise to do with your children as well. It can be a nice way to identify some of their interests from a young age. You don't have to wait until you're dying to check items off your bucket list and find your edge. You'll know when you find it because it feels like your soul is on fire, like you're carving down the mountain at full speed with the wind at your back. You have to chase your passion like it's the last chair lift to the top of the mountain. What are you waiting for?

Made in the USA
Monee, IL
16 May 2021